Praise for

"A story of life, beauty, passion and loss."
—**Christina Marfice**, *Boise Weekly*

"*Anything Worth Doing* unfolds with an inevitability worthy of two vastly different art forms: whitewater dory navigation, and Greek tragedy. The wonder of these forms is that, in Jo Deurbrouck's able hands (as in Homer's or Euripides'), knowing the fatal outcome in no way diminishes the power of the narrative or the element of surprise. Clancy Reece turns out to be a redneck poet-hero worthy of a not-yet-written ballad by Steve Earle, Jon Barker is no less admirably crazed than Lewis or Clark, and Ms. Deurbrouck has written Western river lovers a white-knuckled adventure classic."

—**David James Duncan**, author of *The River Why*, *The Brothers K*, and the forthcoming *Sun House*

"Deurbrouck skillfully tunes us in to the heart and soul of a rare breed, one for whom a wild mountain river is as absolutely necessary as the river of blood flowing through his own body. "

—**Steven Hawley**, author of *Recovering a Lost River: Removing Dams, Rewilding Salmon, Revitalizing Communities*

"The account of Reece's demise is truly terrifying, but *Anything Worth Doing* is ultimately a profile of one of Idaho's last iconoclast boatmen...Reece comes across as bearish and self-reliant, like a landlocked Thor Heyerdahl or a less militant George Heyduke."

—**Grayson Shaffer**, Senior Editor, *Outside Magazine*

"Anyone who's ever sung along buzzed to the Old Crow Medicine Show line 'If I die in Raleigh, at least I will die free' will love this story, as will anyone who has ever known and been quickened by the feral spirits of wild people in love with wild places, and anyone who has ever sat beside a river and pondered the water's beauty and brute strength, and anyone who wants to be transported by a landscape and a story rooted in the physical world."

    —**Chris Dombrowski**, *Missoula Independent*

"*Anything Worth Doing* begins in contemplative headwaters and builds into a story as powerful as a floodstage river."

    —**Rocky Barker**, Author of *Scorched Earth: How the Fires of Yellowstone Changed America*

Sundog Book Publishing, Idaho Falls, ID, USA
www.sundogbookpublishing.com

Cover design by DJ Calderwood
Maps and interior design by B. Rabin
Photos courtesy of Jon Barker

Library of Congress Control Number: 2012935864

Library of Congress Subject Headings
    Adventure and adventurers -- United States -- Biography
    Rafting (Sports)--West (U.S.)
    Rafting (Sports) -- Salmon River (Idaho)
    Salmon River (Idaho) - Description and Travel
    Boatmen -- United States -- Biography

ISBN:
    978-0-9852578-0-4 (pbk.)
    978-0-9852578-1-1 (ebook, .mobi)
    978-0-9852578-2-8 (ebook, .epub)

SUNDOG

For seventeen years now, I've been a boatman. I take people down whitewater rivers in the West. Through the summer, I pretty much live on the river. Set up a kitchen at a different camp each night, lay out a bedroll to sleep on the river bank above the river running, below the stars shining.

I'm supposed to be there. I feel very much at home, at ease and comforted, between the songs of the birds and water and the silence of the stones and the canyon.

—Clancy Reece

Anything Worth Doing

A true story of adventure, friendship and tragedy
on the last of the West's great rivers

Jo Deurbrouck

SUNDOG

> At the beginning of the 19th century, the river systems of the West were still being 'discovered.' By the end of the 20th all had been remade.

As late as the 1930s, the West, with its snowcatching mountain ranges and huge basins, was still a land of mighty rivers. In the Northwest, the Columbia roared through its spring melt season, drawing its icy waters from an entire region. During flood, it replenished sediments, shaping and feeding the land. It flushed salmon and steelhead smolts to the sea by the millions. By late summer, it warmed and subsided to a relative trickle, but even then its waterfalls and rapids were formidable—when they weren't impassable.

It took 14 mainstem dams to chain the Columbia, but the job is done: The river's natural rhythms have been erased. It now works 24 hours a day, 365 days a year, supplying power, navigation, irrigation, and flood control.

All of the Columbia's significant tributaries are also dammed. But those tributaries have tributaries, and although some of these are dewatered for irrigation and agricultural runoff makes others smell like chemistry labs, many, above their rendezvous points with modern river management, remain free and wild.

Each of these is celebrated and protected by its advocates, but among them, the river at the heart of this book, Idaho's Salmon River, is unique. No other Western river of such length, volume, and gradient survived the 20th century so nearly intact.

The Salmon is the last major river that still dances to natural seasonal rhythms, its bed and banks nearly pristine. It's the last river, not just in the West but across the contiguous 48 states, upon which a person can, with skill and courage, float from headwaters to mouth and, over more than 400 miles, imagine himself in a world humans do not control.

Columbia River Basin

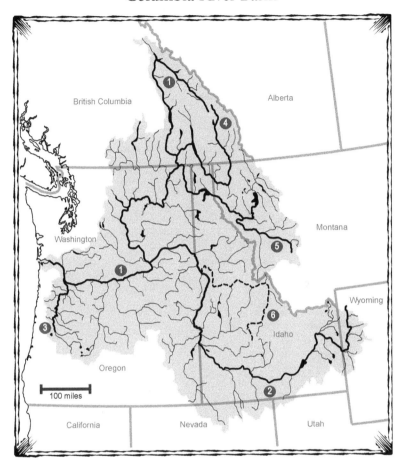

Columbia River and major tributaries:

		length (miles)	average discharge (cubic feet per second)
1.	Columbia	1,243	265,000
2.	Snake	1,078	56,900
3.	Willamette	187	37,400
4.	Kootenay	485	30,650
5.	Pend Oreille/Clark Fork	440	26,430
6.	Salmon (tributary of the Snake)	409	11,060

Salmon River Source to Sea

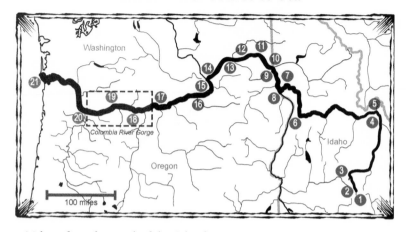

Mileage from the mouth of the Columbia River:

1. Salmon River headwaters: mile 920
2. Source to Sea launch site: mile 912.3
3. Stanley, ID: mile 890.4
4. Salmon, ID: mile 770.7
5. North Fork, ID: mile 748.4
6. Riggins, ID: mile 598
7. Slide Rapid: mile 515.2
8. mouth of the Salmon River (Snake River confluence): mile 511.3
9. Asotin, WA: mile 469
10. Clearwater River confluence, Lewiston, ID: mile 462.2
11. Lower Granite Dam: mile 430.5
12. Little Goose Dam: mile 393.3
13. Lower Monumental Dam: mile 364.6
14. Ice Harbor Dam: mile 332.7
15. mouth of the Snake River (Columbia River confluence): mile 323
16. McNary Dam: mile 292
17. John Day Dam: mile 216
18. The Dalles Dam: mile 192
19. Bonneville Dam: mile 146.1
20. Portland, OR: mile 101
21. Columbia River Bar, Pacific Ocean: mile 0

Salmon River Speed Run

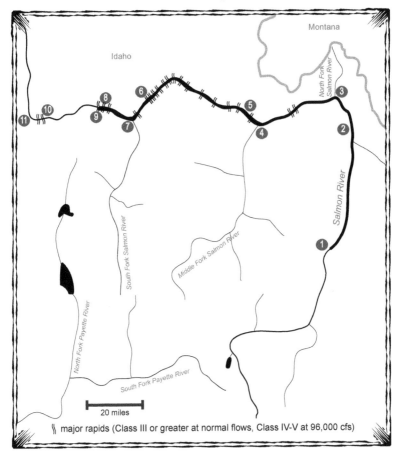

Mileage from the mouth of the Salmon River:

1. Deer Gulch launch site: mile 302.7
2. Salmon, ID: mile 259.4
3. North Fork, ID: mile 237.1
4. Middle Fork Salmon River confluence: mile 198.5
5. Corn Creek boat ramp (end of road from North Fork): mile 190.7
6. Whiplash Rapid: mile 147.3
7. South Fork Salmon River confluence: mile 133.9
8. Chittam Rapid: mile 112.4
9. Vinegar Creek boat ramp (end of road from Riggins): mile 112.3
10. Spring Bar: mile 96.9
11. Riggins, ID: mile 86.7

Preface

Direct experience is our best teacher, but it is exactly what we are most bent on obliterating, because it is so often painful. We grow more comfortable at the price of knowing the world, and therefore ourselves.

—Joe Kane, *Running the Amazon*

We called our home the Blue Ghetto. Each spring it accreted along both sides of a dirt road you could walk the length of in two minutes. Our scrap of road collided at one end with the backside of Three Rivers Lodge, the rustic resort that largely comprised the town of Lowell, Idaho. The other end was swallowed by a wall of dense, dark, dripping green: the Clearwater National alongside, screened from view by willow and syringa, ran the Lochsa (pronounced LOCK-saw). This mountain river swells each spring with snowmelt and rainfall, pounds through dozens of powerful rapids in a handful of miles, and then, just downstream of the lodge, folds with deceptive peace into an even better known mountain river, the Selway.

The denizens of the Blue Ghetto were whitewater raft guides, many of us *career* guides, as we liked to point out to one another. We were not working summer jobs until something better came along. We were living the life. We might not own much, but neither were we owned. We might not be eligible for credit cards—people without permanent addresses tend not to be—but credit cards looked like bad magic, the real-life lamp with the prankster genie inside.

So the 'ghetto' in Blue Ghetto was ironic. We were proud of our poverty and what it bought.

The blue was literal. On the Lochsa in the spring it rains and rains. So we strung cheap blue plastic tarps over our campsites like so many miniature blue skies. The twilight shadows that pooled beneath turned even our faces blue.

It was a glorious mess. Our cheek-by-jowl camps were mud-sticky and puddle-mined, encircled by shallow trenches we dug to divert water around our tents and cooking areas. Some of us slept on salvaged wooden pallets, others in trucks backed up to the ubiquitous tarps. We built shelves and tables out of waste lumber and driftwood. All of it was festooned with boating gear that seldom dried.

As you might expect, our tiny enclave was well endowed with colorful characters. There was Dave, who was in his mid-20s but had yet to own a car. In fact he didn't know how to drive. He hitch-hiked to every destination he couldn't reach by bicycle, including the Lochsa and, somehow or another, Tibet.

There was Lonnie, who had a Master's degree in something I could never remember, although I occasionally heard him mention it to curious guests. An accomplished storyteller, Lonnie liked to kick off his sandals before beginning a tale. Then he'd scuff his feet into the grass or sand as though cleaning a battery terminal. Hooked to his source, still silent, he'd fold his body into an angular origami squat and swivel his long neck until he had captured every eye. Then he'd begin.

There was Carol, in her late 20s with thick dark hair that she kept in elaborate cornrows and ropy braids. She chewed tobacco and sang like a whiskey-bent angel. Her laugh was easy and raucous. You could hear it clear across the river. Despite the tobacco-flecked teeth, weathered skin and bulging biceps, the impression she left in her wake was that a mischievous child had just skipped by.

We played a drinking game there at Three Rivers. Orders from above said guests were not to know about it or, better yet, that we were not to play it. But orders from above felt optional at ground level, and the game thrived.

It went like this: At day's end, any guide who had flipped a boat in the rapids owed the other guides a 12-pack of beer, deliverable upon our return to Three Rivers. But if a guide dumptrucked, in other words if his guests went swimming but the raft remained upright and the guide himself managed to stay onboard, the other guides owed *him* a 12-pack.

It was of course the dumptruck bit our boss did not want guests to hear about. He said it sounded as though we *liked* to see guests in the water. He had a point, so we humored him enough to stop chortling about free beer after such 'carnage' occurred. But we didn't stop playing. We called a guide's post-flip walk to the resort store 'the walk of shame.' We did not stop chortling about that.

Rafting company clientele run rivers for lots of reasons, but our guests, the people who had picked the Lochsa, wanted a wild ride. On the ride upstream to our launch, we passed photo albums around the bus, taken by the company that shot souvenir white-water pictures for us. We told the guests they'd be starring in that afternoon's slideshow. The images in the albums were of rafts twisting into the air as though propelled by land mines; rafts dumping their human contents into roiling chaos; rafts plowing so hard into boulders that they folded themselves into bulbous, 15 foot-long L shapes. Carnage pays, we liked to say. And on the Lochsa it did.

But this book is not about the Blue Ghetto or the Lochsa. Nor is it about me, except indirectly. The reason for describing all this—the Ghetto, those guides—is because if you stand there with me, on that muddy dirt road beside that lovely wild river, you'll see how we might have felt ourselves special, exempt in some way from rules that bind other lives. Not that we would say so and not that we thought ourselves invincible. That's different. Occasionally a guide blew out a knee in a violent paddleboat toss or split a lip on the back of a guest's helmet. You expected that.

But picture it. We threw ourselves at that wild river every day and most days it tossed us all harmlessly skyward like well-loved children. After a while that does something to you.

What this book *is* about is a subculture that still, in memory, charms me. It's about two men named Clancy Reece and Jon Barker, two of the most fascinating boatmen that subculture produced. It's about freedom, adventure, death, and those rare people who, like Clancy and Jon, never *unchoose* simple lives defined by such harsh and lovely bargains.

I remember exactly when I began to unchoose that life, or at least that's what I thought for many years. Looking back from here, I realize I'd never completely accepted its tradeoffs. I was standing in a phone booth outside of Three Rivers Lodge, staring blankly at the

Lochsa while a stranger's voice explained why my friend Jim Yetter hadn't rejoined me at Three Rivers as we'd planned.

The next day I received a letter. J. Yetter, Banks, Idaho, said the envelope's upper left corner. I watched the hand which held the envelope begin to shake. Because what the voice on the phone the previous day had told me was that Jim was dead.

Long-limbed, blond and beautiful, Jim had been a guide for another Lochsa company. He had taken a boatman's holiday to kayak the infamous North Fork of the Payette River. There he had drowned.

This was perhaps my second summer as a guide. As an inexperienced oarsman, I worked family trips on moderate, class III rivers. Class III whitewater can look intimidating to the uninitiated, but its obstacles require no great skill to avoid. The waves can be large but they are predictable. Class III is where whitewater guides cut their teeth.

I had been sent to the Lochsa to see what serious paddle boating looked like and, presumably, so the boss could see if I had class IV-V potential. The Lochsa exhilarated and intimidated me. It was the real thing, a whitewater river that required skill and attention and even a bit of luck. What I had heard about the class V North Fork, where Jim had gone to play, was that it was tougher even than the Lochsa.

In his letter, Jim had written that he had broken his paddle that day in a tough rapid. In water so churned it seemed mostly air, he'd been forced to wet exit from his kayak and swim for shore through a mass of wave-pounded boulders. He didn't know how he had escaped injury. The next day, he wrote, if he could find someone willing to boat it with him, he would try the section boaters call the Middle Five. I didn't know it then, but the Middle Five is the most difficult, dangerous stretch of the North Fork. Plenty of North Fork kayakers won't run it.

Jim did find a paddling partner for the Middle Five. Everything went well with their run until the last rapid, and what went wrong there nobody will ever know because the other paddler didn't see it. What he saw when he turned around at the bottom of the rapid was Jim's kayak completing the run upside down. When Jim didn't exit the kayak or roll upright after what seemed more than enough time, the guy paddled over and spun the boat up. Empty cockpit.

After a frantic search the paddler located Jim, probably alive at first, but only in a technical sense because Jim Yetter would never get the chance to breathe again. He was wedged under a submerged log three feet beneath the surface. The way the story came down the grapevine, the guy could reach Jim with his fingertips but couldn't budge him. He couldn't budge the log either. At some point he scrambled up onto the highway for help, which is the same as saying he surrendered to inevitability. Every whitewater boater knows the rule: one minute to unconsciousness, five to almost certain brain damage, then death.

It was evening before the body was retrieved. By then Jim's letter was on its way to me.

There is a part of that letter I will never forget. Among the talk of broken paddles and nasty swims, Jim had written this: "I'm having the time of my life."

That autumn I drove to the North Fork, found the rapid he had died in, and climbed down the steep bank to the water's edge. I opened the letter and reread that line. By now I could find it in an instant, below the second worn fold on page two. Then I slipped the letter, which had grown too precious to carry, into a crack between two rocks. Standing there, I promised myself that someday I too would kayak the North Fork.

I had never kayaked a class V river. Nor had I thought much

about whether I cared to, except that it was what good boaters did and I intended one day to be good.

I did eventually keep that promise and run the North Fork. Up or off, as climbers say, and by that time I'd been guiding for some five years and was a full-fledged Lochsa guide as Jim had been. Few women worked the Lochsa in my day, but I'd studied and practiced that style of river, then worn my boss down to a definite maybe, then demonstrated the necessary skill.

I did my job on the Lochsa competently. I had no more than my share of swimmers, several perfectly glorious dumptrucks, and no guest injuries more severe than a bloodied nose. But I often guided lightheaded with fear. Some nights I dreamed a swimmer from my raft had been sucked under a log and no matter how hard I tried I could only brush his inert form with my fingertips.

Evenings after work, a few of the guides would load their kayaks and drive back up to a rapid called Pipeline, the heart of which is a powerful surf wave. I seldom went, although I envied whatever in them drew them back to a river which had released them for the day. Or what wasn't in them. Because I assumed without asking that unlike me, they felt no fear.

Then one day a young man tumbled from my paddle boat into a big 'hydraulic' below a rock. Boaters have many names for such hydraulics but the most common is 'hole' because of the way these river features tend to yank anything at the surface down. Strong holes also cycle currents back up and then roll them under again, so the experience of swimming a hole is sometimes described as getting 'washing machined.'

The whole thing happened, as crises do when you have mentally rehearsed them, within a curious stretching of time. The raft dropped over the submerged boulder that created the hole, caught, and then began to buck. Five of my paddlers tumbled onto the floor.

The sixth began to tip toward the most powerful part of the hole.

I had what seemed years to decide that this soon-to-be swimmer was, for the moment, more important than my pummeled raft or the paddlers jumbled inside. I slammed my paddle blade under a thwart and lunged to hook the shoulder of his lifejacket. My hand wrapped solidly around fabric.

It was a nasty hole. If I had missed my grab he'd have been yanked under like a fishing bobber. He'd have been released—keeper holes exist but they are rare and this was not one of them—but not before he completed a scary and perhaps painful swim. That solid handful of fabric said he'd be back in the boat before he could register that he was wet.

But that's not what happened.

My swimmer was yanked under so hard that I was pulled half out of the raft after him, my arm submerged to the shoulder. His sunny yellow helmet was an indistinct greenish blob in the aerated mess of the hole. What held us both was my leg, which I had jammed into the gap between the thwart and the boat's inflated floor so hard I would later find bruises.

I yelled my paddlers back to their places. In moments they began to dig hard at the boiling water. From my awkward position I pulled for perhaps 15 seconds but I might as well have been trying to haul a tree from the ground.

Holes tend to hold most fiercely to objects at the surface because that's where the currents are in greatest conflict—which meant that although my raft was caught, my swimmer didn't have to be. I was holding him in that hole. I began, silently, to count. I hated the thought, but at ten I planned to let go and give him to the river while he still had the strength to swim. The hole would pull him down, but it was weakest in its depths. He'd be released into downstream current and then his lifejacket would haul him back to the surface and he'd be rescued by the rafts waiting below.

I was on four when the paddlers won us free. An instant later the young man popped to the surface. I hauled him from the water and dumped him onto the floor of the raft where he lay, sans pants and one shoe, gasping and coughing. His eyes flew open and he stared at me, in the grip of an emotion I had never before seen but instantly recognized: mortal terror.

That look rattled me, but when I told the story I made the whole thing into a joke, on him for thinking that losing his pants comprised a brush with death, and on me for allowing my boat to run one of the biggest holes in the river in the first place.

I was still special that day, one of the charmed, if just barely. Then in June of 1996, word ripped through the guiding community that another of ours was dead. The next thing we heard was that he'd been one of the old timers, a real dinosaur.

Word was that the guy had been on a boatman's holiday as well, only his was a high water run down Idaho's longest wilderness river, the Salmon. The Salmon is not normally a difficult river, but this was a booming high water year. On the Lochsa we'd been canceling trips for safety.

Extreme high water or not, the news didn't make sense. Rivers are notorious for slamming the foolish ass over teakettle and even more notorious for giving the undeserving a pass. But although we all paid lip service to water's caprice, none of us believed in our hearts that rivers killed the respectful, which we all said we were, and especially not the consummately skilled, which is what it meant to say the man was a dinosaur. Maybe we even thought the river might respect such an oarsman in return.

Then I heard the victim's name: Clancy Reece. A dinosaur's dinosaur. The guy who'd taught the people who had taught me. Their hero and mine. I had known him only to say hello to at boat ramps, but like everyone in Idaho rafting at the time, I knew the Bunyanesque stories. I knew—hell, everyone knew—that Clancy loved a challenge. People were saying that he and a lifelong friend, a serious adventure boater named Jon Barker, had been trying to set some kind of world record.

And someone said this: He must have been having the time of his life.

I guided for several more summers, but that day I realized there would be an end to it for me. I was not a career guide after all. I know now that there are very few career risk takers of any stripe. Most people hedge their bets.

Years later I went to hear a climber and extreme snowboarder named Stephen Koch. After his slideshow—full of edgy images of him flying down chutes steep as rainspouts, walled by ragged rock or empty air—an audience member asked why he took such risks. He'd been nearly killed in an avalanche on Wyoming's Grand Teton. Despite injuries which included a broken back, he was snowboarding extreme terrain again within a year. Since then he'd attempted an alpine-style ascent of Everest, just he and a few friends traveling light and moving fast. That's not how Everest is usually attempted. Because of the likelihood of mishap in that extreme elevation environment, Everest is nearly always approached siege-style, with a virtual army of backup personnel and gear. Yet despite those precautions the mountain still kills at least two climbers in a typical year. Unexpected storms have been known to wipe Everest hopefuls off the roof of the world by the handful. How could Koch say he valued his life, the audience member asked, if he took such risks with it?

By then I was pushing 40. Risk had become a complicated word for me, all tangled up with dreaming and doing, compromise and cost.

"I do not risk my life," Stephen answered. "I take risks in order to live. I take risks because I love life, not because I don't."

Listening to the reaction of the crowd, which ranged from boisterous whistles of approval to dissatisfied silence, and feeling that entire range echo in me, I realized how badly I wanted to write about Clancy Reece. I wanted to write about lives balanced between freedom and risk, lives founded on what at the time seemed to me a fantasy—that childhood wouldn't end, that the bill would never come due.

Most of all I wanted to know whether, if Clancy could have looked at the path of his life in hindsight, as I could, he would have—or could have—unchosen any of it.

Part I

One

A Box Full of Words

In 2002 when I began researching the man Clancy Reece, there was still a telephone listing in that name although its owner had been dead since 1996. It rang in the home Clancy is said to have loved, the only piece of property he ever owned, perched above the Clearwater River in tiny Lenore, Idaho.

Clancy's aging mixed-breed dog, Parts (as in part this and part that), still lived there. So did a large man with meaty, rolled shoulders and a heavy brow, his resemblance to Clancy strong enough that a visitor who had met the house's former inhabitant might be excused for thinking the place haunted.

Charles, Clancy's youngest brother, was 50 when I met him, the age at which Clancy had died. He lived among the remains of another man's life and was clearly proud to do so, sharing the house not just with the man's dog, but also his books, magazines, cats, descendants of cats, grapevines, wine-making gear, rolled-up raft and fishing gear. The family joke was that the house belonged to Parts, who allowed Charles to live there.

As I pulled up, I was certain I was lost. The place appeared uninhabited. This look is not unique in Lenore. More a tumble of small structures than a town, Lenore's primary reason for existence is a grain elevator, also apparently abandoned.

But this house was more dilapidated than most. You could imagine that if you pulled open the front door the structure would exhale a tired, mouse-shit scented sigh and subside to the ground. Except there was no front door. Weathered plywood sheeting was nailed over the gap where a door had once hung. Two front windows were also boarded. The others, cobweb-draped, framed an uninviting blackness. The paper shingles that had served as siding were scraped away here and there like the scales of a spawned-out salmon. In fact the whole property, which included a falling-down storage shed, a yardful of disintegrating household appliances, an old camping trailer, a scattering of ladders, and a slanted, muddy yard, appeared poised to crumble into the Clearwater.

As it turned out, Charles didn't actually live in the ruined house. Neither had Clancy. Home was a low cinderblock building behind the house. From outside it looked like a toolshed, but inside it was a storybook outlaw hideaway, comfortably cluttered and cave-like, foggy with cigarette smoke. It was furnished with an old plaid couch and coffee table, a couple chairs, a microwave and, since it was November, the ticking warmth of a wood-burning cook stove.

Charles was a roofer by trade, good with tools and wood but not known in his family for being good at life. After Clancy's death, the family had given him his big brother's house. Forty-four at the time, he'd never owned much. When his brother-in-law, Tom, had told Charles that the house was his because Clancy had said that if anything ever happened to him it should be, it had felt so good it hurt.

Clancy had intended to renovate the little hideaway but had never gotten around to it. Charles wanted to carry out those plans in his brother's memory, but it felt like a sacred trust. He feared getting it wrong. He'd added a few things, though, including a door for the tiny bathroom and carpet for the concrete slab floor. He'd brought in a bed (Clancy had slept on the floor). He'd also paneled the tiny living room with fine-grained red fir pulled from the interior walls of the old house out front. You can't buy wood like that anymore, he told me. Wood like that comes from the hearts of massive old trees, and the massive old trees are all gone.

Clancy had ripped the lovely red fir from the house's interior walls too, but not to panel his hideaway. He'd burned it for winter heat. Given enough time, the man might have consumed the whole house, a slow demolition which only the tiny cinderblock shack would have survived.

When he'd come here after his brother's funeral, Charles had found the little cave scattered with photos, correspondence, jotted notes, poems, stories and undated journals. He couldn't make himself read them. But he'd carefully gathered every scrap, smoothed the wrinkles, and sorted them into three boxes. One box contained photos, another letters and cards. The third was filled with Clancy's own writing. Poems, notes and journals had apparently been scrawled across whatever was at hand when a thought struck, be it faded yellow tablets, old envelopes, the backs of phone bills or tax notices.

On the phone I had asked for a couple hours, but Charles Reece said he had all day. We sat and he began to talk. While he talked he drank, beer after beer the way a chain smoker consumes cigarettes, each dispatched the same way. He popped the tab, sucked out a mouthful, refilled the can with tomato juice, sucked away the pinkish foam extruding from the hole, then took another swallow. Between swallows, through a curtain of mustache and with such minimal movement of his lips that his words were a riverine mumble, came the stories.

These stories were self-deprecating when about himself, wry but admiring about his brother. They were about bad-boy childhoods in the mill town of Lewiston, Idaho, which in Charles' stories sounded like a lawless 19th century frontier outpost. They were about fishing and rivers and a family that places high value on honor and courage, but little on the letter of the law. In one story, Clancy thrashed his mouthy baby brother for saying something disrespectful, a beating which Charles, even before the bruises faded, decided he had deserved. I grew skilled at deciphering his mumble and the short fall day evaporated.

By evening, Charles had an answer to my first question of the morning: Would he allow me to borrow those three boxes of photos, letters and poems? He had decided to loan me Clancy's doodles, as he called the writing that filled the third box. I couldn't have the photos because I would be leaving with plenty that mattered to him already. I couldn't even peek in the letters box because those letters were personal and nobody's business, not even his.

As I was leaving, Charles, as steady as if all those juice-laced beers had been water, hugged me with real warmth. Then he mumbled that he'd track me down and kill me if I didn't take good care of that box.

Back home days later I stared at the box's contents, the flower and fruit of a largely solitary mind. This was a man who had lived the life I once wanted, who had enjoyed a lifelong freedom many would say they envy. He had been admired by nearly all who had known him. To some he was the real thing, a larger-than-life hero. He had died, as they said, doing what he loved. And this box was full of his words. If there was a way in which the man himself survived, not as a legend or a cautionary example but as himself, it was in that box.

Slightly uncomfortable—how often are we given such unedited glimpses into the minds of private people?—I read every word on every page. It took an entire day.

Yellow pads were filled with journal entries, written in a loose hand that skipped alternate lines and talked to an unspecified 'you,' mostly about rivers and river trips and boats. Pithy, bumper sticker-like epigrams occupied the backs of old phone bills and shopping lists, reminding me of something I'd heard from Clancy's friends. They had said he spoke seldom, but when he did you often wished for pen and paper. Did he collect or invent his epigrams, study them so they would be on the tip of his tongue when needed? Was his off the cuff wisdom more calculated than his admirers supposed?[*]

I wouldn't want to step on you barefoot.

If none of the answers are right maybe the question is wrong.

As long as you don't see why I'm right and you're wrong, you can't hope to claim you understand the situation.

We arm ourselves with nets of logic and try to catch the waters of truth.

---

[*] I struggled with whether Clancy's writing belonged in this book. His mother and two of his brothers thought so, and in the end, so did I. Since all Clancy left were jotted notes clearly not intended for publication, I've cleaned up spelling and punctuation when doing so didn't significantly alter meaning. Otherwise, here and throughout the book, Clancy's words are as I found them in the box Charles handed to me that day in Lenore.

Authority is something to resort to when intelligence has failed.

Drug laws trample on the principle that the pursuit of happiness is an inalienable right.

I am what I am. If that isn't what you want, you want the wrong thing.

There were also descriptions of simple, clever inventions: a fishing rod holder; a vise-griplike way to mount an outboard onto a fishing boat's transom; an insect harvester to draw insects to what Clancy called "points of use," particularly fish hatcheries; a handwritten ad selling instructions for a minnow trap made from a plastic pop bottle. Readers were supposed to send "Clancy the Boatman" $4.25 for the design. The minnow trap's instructions included the admonition that it would be "bad manners and bad medicine" if the trap were lost, because plastic biodegrades slowly and the decomposing water creatures trapped inside would attract live ones, "killing critters for years and years."

"Thank you once for buying my trap," Clancy had concluded. "Thank you twice for using it with conscience."

There were business plans, but none that had been carried past preliminaries. In one, Clancy argued for opening the Little Salmon—a rollicking tributary to the Salmon River with a short and unpredictable season—to commercial whitewater rafting. In another, he proposed a flyfishing/historical tourism business on the Clearwater River between the tiny old logging and mining town of Orofino and Lewiston, Territorial Idaho's first capitol. He planned to call his company "Clarence Clearwater Revisals."

Several letters and documents from other people had crept into the mass. One was from a woman named Eldene Wasem. It was addressed to Clancy's mother. Its subject was an auto accident in June of 1979. Apparently Clancy, an EMT, had been first on the scene of Eldene's wreck. The woman wrote, "I had tried for so long to find the nice person that helped me from the wreck. You have a son to be proud of." Another letter was from river guests. It said they were giving Clancy a copy of Hemingway's *In Our Time*, because even though he had probably read the Big Two-Hearted River stories about a solitary trout fisherman, Clancy might not own his own copy and should.

But it was the poems I read again and again. There were dozens. I tried to guess if they were all his or if some were copied from other sources. I decided I heard one voice and one attitude behind them. I pondered my feeling that, although some of the poems addressed the whole mistaken world, most seemed aimed at a beloved other. Although Clancy wrote silly songs that he performed for friends and guests on river trips, to my knowledge these more thoughtful poems never left his tiny cave until Charles handed me the 'doodles' box. In researching this book, I didn't meet anyone who mentioned knowing that Clancy wrote poetry.

I wondered who he had been writing for. I tried to picture the big man in his ascetic's shack above the Clearwater—passionate, frustrated, blissful, perhaps lonely but certainly free—explaining himself to paper instead of people. Was that how it was? Although people described him as a warm and genuine friend, he was also a lover of solitude with a reputation for walking away from women as though departing a restaurant after a good meal. Did he write what he would not say for fear that he would be followed home and lose his precious solitude? Or was there someone to whom he read these poems, someone I didn't find in my research because my interest was in Clancy the whitewater raft guide, Clancy the iconoclast, Clancy the hermit, and you tend to find what you seek? Or because she—or they—were as private as Clancy himself?

When we total and tally
the treasures of men
I can say that you kissed me
and smiled, and kissed me again.

So they cursed you
in their madness
and they hurt you
in their sadness

now forgive them
in their sorrow

and love them
in their folly

for it's much the same
as yours.

When you send young men to war
Who stay must count this in the score,
that when they come back from that war
They can be young men nevermore.

Lie next to me and warm me
because the night is cold

I don't ask because I want your love—

It's just—the night is cold

It's not because your downcast eyes
and half a smile upon your lips
leave an empty feeling in my mind
and an ache beneath my ribs

no, it's none of that at all—
It's just—the night is cold.

They say men judge others
by themselves.
I think that's probably true.
I hope you'll give some thought
to what you just told me about you.

Paging back, I pictured the tired little town of Lenore in its pretty river canyon. Clancy had pointed out in one of his incomplete business proposals that, of the waterways Lewis and Clark traveled on their famous journey 200 years before, the upper Clearwater is the only one that still flows free. An hour upstream of Lenore, the Clearwater's parent rivers, the Lochsa and Selway, meet. Each remains as wild as the grizzlies which still wander its banks.

Thanks to those free mountain rivers, the Clearwater above its first mainstem dam still swells with snowmelt, then clarifies as it falls over the long, warm summers. Thanks to fish ladders, hatcheries, and a barging program that transports salmon and steelhead around the many dams downstream, the Clearwater still hosts remnants of the great runs that once were bedrock to both ecosystem and economy. The river that runs silent by this forgotten town—a cold, rich artery beneath muscular bluffs—is a flowing reminder of a time when big rivers and their inexorable rhythms ruled the region.

And the poet who scribbled here, did he choose this place for such powerful reasons as these? Was he the man so many of his admirers saw, a man who would not be owned? Or was he an ineffectual dreamer, carried to this sad scrap of a town by the random currents of an unplanned life? I knew from documents found in that box that the annual property tax on his home had totaled less than $70, a sum easily made in a half-day's guiding, and that he had failed to pay it three years running. I found myself wanting to see this as a Thoreaulike statement. I wanted the man in that box to have been a dreamer, yes, but a fiercely pragmatic one, a man for whom it made perfect sense to rip a house apart for firewood rather than take a winter job and be forced away from his thoughts and his beloved river.

Two

A Head Full of Projects

July, 2002

"These are my secrets," wails Jon Barker, only half-kidding. "You'll think I'm a whacko."

We sit at his dining table before a cobwebbed picture window that looks onto rolling farmland. No other houses are visible, which is how he likes it.

Jon is 40. He's not a big man, but he's got a quick, confident way of moving I associate with people who have lived an outdoor life. His dark hair is clipped short except for a pencil-thin braid that hangs down his back. His skin looks smooth and boyish, unusual on a longtime raft guide. One of the things I will notice later, after I leave, is that I'll remember his face as being, most often, still and serious. And yet my notes will be full of funny and self-deprecating things the man said.

In front of us on Jon's dining table are files and stacks of paper. Printouts detail the annual fluctuations of Idaho's Salmon River for nearly a century. Closely handwritten pages list landmarks along this river, each beside its distance—to a tenth of a mile—from the Salmon's confluence with the Snake. Rowing speeds between these points are listed for different flows, different boats, different wind conditions.

Jon likes the idea of a book about the man he calls Clarence or Twerp, and of whom he speaks in the present tense, as though his friend were not six years dead. To Jon Barker, Clarence Reece was—is—the sort of man about whom books *should* be written.

I have told Jon the book will be about him, too. This does not please him as much. Between the pleasure of having people understand his passions and the frustration of trying to make himself understood, frustration weighs more.

I have also told Jon that I envision him and his friend as a modern-day Huck Finn and Tom Sawyer and have entertained myself trying to figure out which is which. This does please him. Jon has thought of himself and Clancy that same way. He doesn't know which is which either.

That's what people will want to hear about, I've told Jon. That and a life in which comfort and security are low priorities. And how Clancy died that day on the Salmon, and whether his death changed the equation for Jon.

So here I sit in the middle of Jon's secrets. Yep, I tell him silently, I think you're a whacko.

These secrets, or projects as Jon more often calls them, are not just on the dining table. One fills a nearby wall. It consists of a photocopied, pieced-together topographic map representing 100 miles of the Snake River, including that river's deepest, most rugged stretch, Hells Canyon. Here and there on this map, hand-drawn V shapes in orange highlighter slice across the closely spaced topographic lines that trace the canyon's steep, basalt slopes. These highlighter V's mark completed hikes.

Jon's plan is to walk every single one of the canyon's prominent ribs from the river to its divide, the point at which melting snow would drain into a different basin. There are more than 200 such ribs to be hiked, each rising at least 2,000 feet and in a few cases as many as 7,000 feet above the river. Jon usually hikes them alone, moving quickly. Often he runs back down. He sometimes wears a lifejacket in case, on his return to the river, it makes more sense to swim than hike downstream to camp. The lifejacket also comes in handy when he gets the chance to hitchhike on a passing raft or jetboat.

Jon likes to imagine what his map will look like when it is complete, when hundreds of thin orange lines reach up from a river corridor so heavily traveled by rafters and fishermen that it hardly seems like wilderness, into rugged country seldom seen by anyone. One day, he says, he will know something nobody else knows. He will know what a man can see from every significant ridge on that 100 miles of river.

On a dining room wall is another pieced-together map. This one is a seven and a half minute topo, which means that each square mile of land is represented on the map by a two inch block. Like all topos, it sketches not just roads and other man-made features, but also the vertical detail of the terrain.

"This is a picture of the earth that surrounds this house," says Jon.

On the map, tributaries of the Clearwater River extend like tree roots into the flat white that denotes the local farmland. One of these roots passes just south of this house. It's called Six Mile Canyon. It's part of another of Jon's projects.

Six Mile is nothing like the big whitewater rivers where Jon spends most of his time. It's tiny and short. Often it's dry. Navigating it will involve as much boat-dragging and bush-bashing as paddling. On the other hand, it has probably never been run. Besides Jon, who would want to?

First descents of major rivers, like first ascents of big mountains, have long compelled adventurers. But there are few such rivers remaining in the world, rivers whose romance lies in the fact that they have so far rebuffed explorers either with their violence, their inaccessibility or their remoteness. Those that remain will almost certainly surrender to full scale, well-funded expeditions.

Six Mile, however, will surrender to Jon Barker, who will run the decidedly unromantic trickle in a kayak, probably alone. Even during peak runoff, Jon figures he'll have to walk at least the last couple miles, perhaps more if the tiny waterfalls along its brush-filled length are not navigable. He will exit Six Mile where it flows into Big Canyon Creek, which is neither much of a canyon nor particularly big, and doesn't even offer the challenge of waterfalls. Gravelly and sedate, Big Canyon Creek was once on Jon's project list but he ran it six years ago.

The project that drags him down those bush-choked little creeks started when, in his twenties, Jon decided he'd run 20 new stretches of river each year. They didn't have to be first descents, but they had to be new to him.

As he ran out of well-known rivers, he had to bushwhack into increasingly obscure streams in order to make his quota. The thought that some of these were de facto first descents amused him. So he began looking for even more unlikely targets, upping the probability that nobody in their right mind would have tried them.

Jon occasionally talks friends into coming—Clancy joined him on a few of these—but mostly he goes alone. Second invitations to these creek-baggings tend to be declined.

At the kitchen table, Jon takes a phone call and I wander away. Upstairs I find a small room around whose walls march cardboard boxes full of maps. A four-drawer file cabinet is crammed with more maps. I have watched this man, when talking about a river with a map before him, trace its flowing line with a finger or his eyes. But he also traces the flanks down which its water seeps and through which it percolates, what hydrologists call its catchment. Jon loves the folded, carved land because he loves the rivers it creates and cradles. He loves the rivers because they shape the land. He loves maps because they allow him to hold all of it in his hands.

Besides maps, the most obvious sign that anyone lives in the house is the scatter of hunting and skiing paraphernalia stored here and there against walls. In Idaho, raft guiding is primarily summer work, so Jon guides fall bighorn sheep, deer and elk hunts. In winter he directs the ski patrol and runs the avalanche control program at a ski area near Seattle, Washington, called Alpental.

Maps. Hunting gear. And, oddly, calendars. Calendars hang in almost every room of Jon's house, all at least a year out of date. Which makes sense when I realize they must be gifts—what do you give a guy like Jon for Christmas, a toaster? One such calendar from the year 2000 is called Wild Places. Each month has a quote and a photo. The photos are striking. I expect to like the quotes and, as I page through them, find I do.

> "There are only two kinds of men in the world: those who stay at home and those who do not."
>
> —Rudyard Kipling

> "The greatest poverty in life is not to live in a physical world."
> —Wallace Stevens

There is little other indication that anyone lives here and in a way, no one does. Jon has spent eight days in this house since last November. This is July. There's little furniture, mostly that godawful glass-topped dining table and a living room couch that arrived with a former roommate and stayed on. There's a little snack food in the kitchen, pushed neatly to the back of the counter. The packaging is battered as though it were 'river kill,' leftovers guides salvage as they unpack a raft trip, which it probably is.

There is an odd kind of living clutter here, though. Not of someone going about a life, leaving dirty plates and newspapers in his wake, but the clutter of passions made visible. Walking around this house makes me feel like I'm tiptoeing through someone's brain.

I glance at Jon, off the phone now and back to poring over lists, hydrologic graphs and maps of the Salmon. Lost in his love of encrypted river minutiae, he seems to have forgotten that a stranger is snooping through his house taking notes.

He looks small for a guy who's done so many big things, walked and floated so many unroaded miles, dreamed up so many 'projects.' Small, stocky and unimpressive, especially right now as he hunches over scribbled sheets of paper at a dining table that would be hard to get rid of at a yard sale. The sharp black stare that is his one dramatic feature is not evident now. For a moment I think he's pretending this deep absorption, but my eyes again sweep the maps tacked to every available surface, and I believe it.

"I'm doing what I will always do," the 40-year-old has said. He means immersing himself in rivers, both figuratively and literally, and making his living in desert canyons and mountains. It's a degree of certitude I'd normally laugh at. But standing here in this house, I believe that, too.

Three

Just a Ballet Dancer from Idaho

So now you've met Clarence 'Clancy' Reece and his friend, Jon Barker. They seem an unlikely pair, don't they? The second is driven and, as will soon become clear, is happy to drive others nearly as hard as himself. The first created—and guarded—a life in which nobody drove him, including perhaps himself. The second tunnels singlemindedly through all those projects. The first spent much of his time simply thinking, slowly filling his tiny shack with ideas until scribbled scraps of paper drifted about the place like fall leaves.

At this point in my research I had a problem. I wanted very much to write about the river hermit I'd met in that cardboard box, but except for their shared love of rivers I couldn't see what Jon was doing in Clancy's story. I needed to return to Clearwater country. Here is what I learned.

Clarence Reece was born in 1945 in Lewiston, Idaho, a lumbermill town at the confluence of the Snake and Clearwater rivers. The family was one in which internal tensions that could have pulled its members apart instead cemented them stubbornly, wordlessly together. When I met the family, all but one of four surviving Reece children lived in Idaho. Two remained in the Lewiston area, one next door to their mother, Evelyn, and the other, part-time, in the house in which she'd raised them.

Evelyn's husband had been decades older than she, a gruff logger more comfortable among trees than people, able to muster little patience and less warmth for his family. The work of raising and, twice, burying children fell on the strong shoulders of this woman, raised on the Dakota plains and accustomed to storms and cold.

Evelyn's lost children were not spoken of. Her surviving young were expected to take no crap, make no excuses, and never sass their mother. To this day they don't, and have little tolerance for such character flaws in others.

The streets of Lewiston were the Reece boys' playground. To them laws were like backyard fences. If you were strong enough to vault over or smart enough to crawl under, the law did not apply to you.

Clarence was a scrawny, mouthy kid, his nose always in a book. This earned him both his first nickname, Twerp, and endless harassment from bigger kids. Getting trounced was not in the family credo and he didn't plan to stop reading or mouthing off, so the boy decided to stop being small. At the local Boys Club, Clarence began lifting weights, jumping rope, and working out on a punching bag.

According to family legend, before he was 18 he had remade himself. Now big, muscular and quick for his size, Clarence was a Golden Gloves boxer and a winning high school wrestler. And if it was true what everyone said, that he had read every single book in the school library, well, nobody outside the family seemed to see a problem in that anymore.

Clarence relished his newfound power and held himself to strict if somewhat obscure rules for its use. Once he stopped a group of neighborhood bullies from harassing a smaller boy by pointedly introducing the child to his tormentors as his, Clarence's, friend. At the time, the boy didn't know Clarence. The bigger boy was just another of the town toughs, another potential tormentor. Clarence hadn't told the boy he intended to help, had never really talked to him at all. So when Clarence called him over to the loitering, dangerously bored group, the child hesitated, then finally came, shaking. And passed a test he hadn't known he was taking. Clarence, he later learned, believed that people should earn assistance.

Clarence never asked the boy if the trick worked (it mostly did). However, he did begin teaching the child to box at the local Boys Club.

The Reece boys learned early that although little in the human world came free, the Clearwater River gave generously to the alert. When Clarence's younger brother, Tom, was 12, the Clearwater gave the boy a rowboat. The little craft had nosed ashore, unmanned, at Holbrook Island adjacent to town. Holbrook Island was a good hunting spot for river gifts, especially after spring melt in the years before Dworshak Dam impounded the river's North Fork and, with it, much of the mainstem's high and mighty spring flows. Nobody came asking for the boat. By Reece rules, this made it Tom's.

Not long after, Clarence and three buddies conceived a plan to shove Tom's rowboat into the Clearwater upstream of town, on a stretch where tall but regular waves stacked up one after another, a free roller coaster just waiting for boys bold enough to take the ride.

The river was swollen and cold with snowmelt that day, but the boys were not concerned. This was the early 1960s and recreational whitewater rafting, with its safety procedures and specialized gear, hadn't yet infiltrated public consciousness even in Idaho, the state that would one day bill itself the nation's whitewater capital. In the early 60s, most equipment used on whitewater had been developed by the military primarily for difficult surf landings, and was sold to a tiny, eccentric segment of the public mostly through surplus warehouses. Nobody the boys knew would have been able to look at that small rowboat and warn them that it was not a whitewater craft.

Evelyn Reece's faith in her smart, strong son had become as solid over the course of his growing up as her faith in herself, so when she heard the plan she insisted only that the boys carry inflated inner tubes as life preservers. Even when, hours later, a siren wailed up the river road, she was not concerned.

Then came a knock at the door and Clarence and his friend, Rick, were helped inside by EMTs. Although wrapped in blankets, they shivered miserably. They were thoroughly—and in Clarence's case, uncharacteristically—cowed.

The boys told her they had shoved away from shore and drifted downstream toward the big waves, exactly as planned. But almost immediately the plan began to go wrong. The boat took on water and quickly grew too heavy to maneuver. The boys watched helplessly as their little craft wallowed over the last waves and then, as if reeled by an invisible fisherman, ran straight at one of the concrete pilings supporting the Lenore Bridge. When it hit, it tipped them all into the water.

Flipping a boat doesn't have to be a serious problem but this time it was, first because the boys had no life jackets, those inner tubes having apparently been misplaced; and second because around the next bend was Big Eddy.

Big Eddy was a productive fishing hole, so the Reece boys and their friends knew it well. Folks said the whirlpools generated at its edges could suck a log to the bottom and hold it there. Stories from early in the century told of 60 foot-long, steam-powered stern wheelers spinning helplessly in its powerful currents, unable to break back into downstream flow.

As the boys swept around the curve above Big Eddy, each clutching the swamped boat, they saw horrified expressions on the faces of fishermen on shore. The men began shouting at them. Two of the boys abandoned the boat and broke hard for shore. The current just above the eddy helped by sweeping near the bank, and the two quickly reached safety. Clarence and Rick, determined to save Tom's boat, stayed with it in midstream.

According to those ashore, when they hit the roiling water at the eddy line they simply disappeared, boat and all.

Tense moments ticked by. Neither the boat nor the boys' heads reappeared. Anxious watchers were sure they'd drowned. An ambulance was called. Clarence later told friends he tumbled about in the bowels of that eddy until he, too, believed he was dying.

Neither Clarence nor Rick were able to recall how they made it to shore under their own power, but each of them did. Tom's boat was lost, and although Clarence had risked his life to save it, he made no apology to his little brother for the loss.

Years later, Evelyn Reece heard that Rick had drowned somewhere out in California trying to rescue a woman caught in a riptide. By then, her boy Clarence had become a whitewater raft guide, and Evelyn had begun to suspect that the only things bigger and stronger than her big strong son were the rivers he loved. Rick's distant death, a seeming finish to something begun that day in Tom's rowboat, was final confirmation. Evelyn decided a river would eventually take her son. It couldn't be helped and she wouldn't dwell on it, but when the day came, she would not have the pain of surprise to sharpen the pain of loss.

As Clarence matured, the childhood nickname Twerp some-how stuck, though it now had all the apparent logic of calling a fat man 'Slim.' The young man made doorways look small, a trick of presence as much as size, since although powerfully built, he was only six feet tall. But for those who knew him best, the name still fit the burly young man who could quiet a rowdy bar just by rising to his feet, who didn't object to mashing noses when it seemed war-ranted, but whose favorite threat among family, since he apparently didn't have the most pleasing voice, was, "Careful, or I'll sing to you."

Clarence took boxing seriously through high school and into college. He even studied ballet to improve his footwork in the ring. When he eventually quit boxing he continued to dance. He liked to joke that lifting pretty girls beat hell out of getting punched by sweaty guys.

Then he flunked a French class and lost his college deferment. Across the country, Vietnam was siphoning young men from their hometowns. Clarence was drafted to serve on an oil transport ves-sel, the USS Neches, stationed in the Philippines. His service was relatively uneventful—the Neches operated mostly out of harm's way—but the less-than-welcome home at its end left a bitter taste in his mouth. If the family edict to take no crap had been difficult to cleave to in the Navy, it proved impossible for a veteran of a painful, confusing war.

One of the few stories Clarence liked to tell about his service went like this: One day, as he was working a punching bag aboard ship, a man approached. The man said he handled a competitive boxer who needed to stay sharp. Would Clarence mind sparring? Clarence told the trainer he didn't want to get beat up. The trainer assured him the boxer would take it easy.

After eating several ringing punches, Clarence decided this boxer was taking it anything but easy. He also realized that although the guy was powerful, his big slow swings often left him vulnerable. Clarence began stepping in to land fast flurries of blows, dancing back, stepping in, dancing back. They went three more rounds. Finally the other boxer began to stagger and the trainer called the match.

As Clarence walked away, he heard the trainer call out, "Do you know you just beat up the Navy's middleweight champion?"

Still irritated, Clarence didn't answer.

"Who are you, anyway? Who taught you to box?"

At this Clarence turned back. "Oh, I'm no boxer," he said sweetly. "Just a ballet dancer from Idaho."

His other favorite story was of the night that, steaming toward California, he and several friends snuck into the paint room and mixed up gallons of pink paint. They also borrowed rope. Then they took turns lowering each other from the bow with a bucket and a brush. Clarence's favorite part of the story was the part he could only imagine: the captain's reaction when a radioman ashore hailed the U.S.S. Neches to inquire what the hell a two-story, pink peace sign was doing on the oiler's hull.

Clarence returned from service quieter, more serious, and more certain he wanted to develop his mind. He re-enrolled at Lewis-Clark State College. He was editor of the college newspaper, starred in college plays, and continued to dance. Friends who saw him on stage found the apparent contrast between his tough guy appearance and these pastimes fascinating. Strangers sometimes mistook his inward-leaning silence for the stupidity with which burly men are often credited. If they didn't revise that assumption on their own, Clarence amused himself by coming up with quiet little comments designed to help them out.

But friends from those days also recall that life seemed to feel aimless to Clarence. What the young man had not yet found was the thing he most wanted, a place so right for him that he'd stick like a well-thrown dart into cork, a place that would complete him as the woods had his silent father.

Four

River Roads

In 1970, a man named John 'A.K.' Barker, a theater professor at Lewis-Clark State College in Lewiston, Idaho and an avid outdoorsman, discovered whitewater. A.K. had worked as an amateur ski patroller in winter. He'd led group backpacking trips in summer. His children, including a boy named Jon, had skied almost as soon as they'd walked. But rivers quickly became A.K. Barker's primary recreational passion.

Whitewater recreation had begun on Eastern rivers, but the budding Western whitewater scene was nothing like its parent. Most Eastern whitewater runs can be completed in a few hours. Some of the West's most exciting rivers slice through big wilderness and require days or weeks to complete. Running wilderness rivers requires all the skills of backcountry travel in addition to whitewater skills. The rewards are not just adrenaline and the restless beauty of water, but access to country so wild it seems the river has transported you 100 years backward in time. Best of all, in those early years river traffic was limited, largely because there was no easy way to learn whitewater skills. Almost none of today's guidebooks, schools, specialized maps, magazines, websites and equipment retailers existed.

A.K. learned the way other early rafters did, by diving in. He took a summer job running Idaho and Oregon's Hells Canyon on the Snake River in army surplus rafts mounted with outboard motors. And although few tourists were lining up to buy rides that first summer, A.K. Barker also convinced his employer to let him train his favorite theater student, a huge, quiet, clever young man named Clarence Reece.

Just like that, the younger man's course was set. He talked about graduate school and white collar careers of various flavors, but from that first whitewater job, no matter what else he did, Clarence always returned to rivers. He guided in Idaho, then on the Colorado in the Grand Canyon, most famous of America's wilderness rivers. Then he returned to Idaho, bouncing through several rafting companies before landing a management position in Riggins, Idaho, on the Salmon River.

In those early days when Clarence was becoming established, the profession attracted an odd lot who tended to stumble into rather than aim at their new lives. Bruce Elmquist, for instance, wandered into Snake River country in 1984 on horseback, at the end of a ride which had begun in Portland two years before. A hippie from La Jolla, California, Bruce knew nothing of horses at the start of his journey, but horses were the fallback plan he and a buddy dreamed up when they couldn't afford plan A, about which they had also dreamed in ignorance: a hot air balloon.

Adventures and misadventures later, Bruce Elmquist found

himself working at a backcountry ranch on a remote section of the Snake River called Hells Canyon, where sheep were sheared and wool stomped into bales the back-breaking, old-fashioned way. When the ranch was sold after a couple seasons, Bruce left as he had arrived, on horseback, meandering upcanyon into ever wilder country. He had no plan. He was in no hurry.

One day while he was washing clothes near his riverside camp, a party of rafters pulled ashore. They offered to take him through the rapid just downstream, which they said was called Granite. It is arguably the biggest whitewater ride in Hells Canyon, but Bruce couldn't know that. He knew he had nothing better to do that day, though, he seldom turned down a new experience. They loaned him a lifejacket and he hopped into the raft.

Because the river drops so steeply at Granite, the actual rapid was invisible as the raft drifted toward its lip. Bruce's only clues that something violent lay ahead were the plumes of water rising from below that lip. They looked like whale spouts.

As they drew closer to the drop off, the distant roar he'd heard from his camp grew, gaining such authority that it filled Bruce's head, washing away even his dawning apprehension. The raft skated on the smooth water of the V, the tongue that led, as in most rapids, straight into the meat of the thing. Then the V and its hitchhiker, the raft, fell down a huge glass hill and the ride began in earnest. The raft was buried, tossed skyward, buried and tossed, again and again. Minutes later an awed and exhilarated Bruce was deposited on shore to make his way back to his camp.

When he ran out of supplies Bruce traveled over the Seven Devils Mountains and into Salmon River country. There he met people who got paid to run tourists through rapids like the one that had rocked his world. Bruce hired on and began what he calls "sink or swim" guide training. His boss was a huge, gruff man by the name of Reece.

By the time he hired Bruce Elmquist, Clarence Reece had picked up a new nickname, Clancy. He had been guiding for more than ten years, which in such a young industry conferred minor guru status. His size and silence were intimidating, but Bruce found himself seeking the man out and listening avidly to what Clancy deigned to say. Bruce noticed others did too.

Another 1980s Clancy trainee was Mike Kennedy, a young Nebraska farmer whose love affair with rivers began when he happened to see a *National Geographic* special on Idaho's wilderness whitewater. Mike was so taken with the thought of this wild West river camping thing that he located a raft company's phone number, a minor feat in those pre-internet days, and called about a trip for his family. The price floored him. "Isn't that a lot of money for a *camping* trip?" he asked.

"If you think that's so much money buy your own goddam boat," said the man and hung up.

Mike did exactly that. His first wilderness whitewater trip in his new raft was a disaster. He and his friends chose Idaho's roadless Salmon River because that's where the *National Geographic* adventurers had gone. Every day, again and again, when they heard the river raising its voice around a bend, they rowed to the bank. They had to. What would have been obvious to an experienced boater—the deep, hollow roar of a class IV rapid, the splashing of class II riffles—were all the same to them. Neither could they see how shoreline features telegraphed riverbed changes. So on a river with only a handful of serious rapids, the Nebraskans scouted and scouted, advancing so slowly that they ran out of food days before they regained civilization.

This didn't stop them from returning to Idaho to try again. And again. Adventures and misadventures later, Mike was rowing toward takeout at Riggins, Idaho when a big man, feet planted wide at the water's edge, began bellowing at him.

It took the startled farmer a moment to understand what was happening. This man, who apparently ran a river company, had mistaken Mike for one of his new guides. The man was angry because Mike was rowing into town far too early to have given paying guests a good ride.

When Mike protested that he didn't work for any outfitter, Clancy Reece didn't miss a beat.

"Do you want to?" he said.

Take tourists down the river? Rivers were for getting away from people. "I'd rather shovel shit," Mike shot back.

He returned to Nebraska for haying season, but a few weeks of humidity, hay and heat later, he packed up his belongings and, with a stranger's possibly flippant offer for a landing pad, headed for Idaho. In 2002 when I began researching this book, Mike and his wife Connie still lived and guided on the Salmon River.

Wilderness raft guides of the 70s and 80s were often, like Clancy Reece, Mike Kennedy and Bruce Elmquist, lovers of freedom with a healthy distrust of rules. They were less often looking for employment when they stumbled into guiding than a solution to what, for each, had been a lifelong problem: how to fit into or somehow hide out from the increasingly urban, increasingly fast-paced latter 20th century. Many felt they should have been born into a time with more elbow room, a time in which a man could build a good life from raw materials and honest sweat, call it his own, and fine print be damned.

Many of those early guides had no permanent homes. They'd camp at the company warehouse between trips, sleeping in their cars or among the rolled-up rafts. In winter they'd hire on at a ski area or travel to South America where hoarded summer wages could keep a person until spring.

Western river towns, historically sustained by logging, mining and ranching, began to metamorphose under the weight of all those sport sandals and go-with-the-flow mentalities. This was particularly true in tiny Riggins, where in the early 80s Clancy was managing a brand-new rafting company called Salmon River Challenge. The owner's plan, like others in Riggins, was to sell multi-day wilderness trips on the Lower Salmon. But Clancy had been studying the whitewater-packed stretch of river that ran right past town. He thought it looked perfect for a single-day trip.

Local outfitters and Clancy's own boss disagreed. The whole point of Idaho boating was wilderness, they argued. Clancy pioneered his day trip idea anyway, and it turned out he was right. People who were intimidated or simply didn't have time for a longer trip were happy to play for a single day. The market for a roller coaster was much larger than for a wilderness expedition.

Over the next few years, day trip companies sprang up like mushrooms along Highway 95, which doubled as Riggins' main street. Whitewater and tourism quickly became the town's most important industries, to the disgruntlement of many old timers. Clancy's personal success was short-lived, however. After a falling out with the owner over how he would be compensated for the success of his day trip vision, he left in disgust, his management experiment over.

A.K. and Maryé Barker had two sons, Jon and Jacques, and a daughter, Devon. The boys in particular were fascinated with the family friend, this giant adults handled with care but whose eyes twinkled secret code, and whom young boys could climb like a jungle gym. Clarence had been their childhood hero, everything they thought a man should be. As they grew up, he shrank—or grew—from idol to teacher to friend.

Wilderness raft guiding began changing in the late 1980s as

adventure recreation lost its fringe status. Successful rafting companies now wooed clientele with slick brochures and polished, efficient office staff to answer the phones. Guides were told to cut their hair, wear shirts, bathe, trim their beards. Increasingly, new hires had degrees in outdoor recreation, sports psychology or counseling.

The new goal was to 'package' wilderness adventure into a comfortable, convenient family experience. An encounter with nature, sure, but a controlled one. Guides led hikes and sing-alongs, played guitar, and hosted talent shows. They served multi-course meals accompanied by appropriate wines on tables laid with checkered cloth. There were women's trips, family trips, yoga trips, birders' trips. Guides gave speeches about river history and biota, but few knew the river as you know the thing that lies at the center of your life, because increasingly this new breed of guide came and went in a few years.

Companies developed training programs. Professional guide schools sprang up. The old boatmen had invented their jobs. They'd had no choice. The new guides were taught theirs.

By the time he left Riggins, dinosaurs like Clancy no longer fit the industry they'd helped create. His perfect refuge no longer so perfect, Clancy landed back where he'd started, working with his old friend A.K. Barker on the Salmon and Snake. A.K. had seen the writing on the wall a decade earlier, and had created his own small river company, Barker River Trips, which had no intention of evolving away from its relaxed origins.

Son Jon, as the Barker family sometimes calls him, had been a child in the first, freewheeling days of Western whitewater rafting and guiding. But like his father's generation, he saw himself as a throwback, a man who would have known how to capitalize on a wilder, bigger age. When Clancy Reece, still called Twerp or Clarence by the Barker family, rejoined Barker River Trips, Jon was a young guide-in-training.

Jon's father told me a revealing childhood story about his son. A.K. was leading a group of adults on a backpacking trip in the Selway-Bitterroot wilderness. As he often did, he'd brought Jon. Toward the end of one tiring day's hike, the boy was driving him crazy. Even at seven Jon had more wilderness competence than patience, so to save them both irritation, A.K. sent the boy ahead with the family dog to "the next creek, where we'll camp." The child was told to entertain himself there by gathering firewood.

But Jon had hiked this trail before. He knew a far better camp than the one his dad had in mind. It was only a few miles further. Those grownups couldn't be *that* tired. In his mind, he could see the good camp, its big sand beach backing a pretty cove, and the pack bridge that spanned the river there. A boy could spend a whole evening running across that bridge, feet thumping on the wooden boards, stopping to peer into the glassy river and spy on the trout hanging motionless behind rocks.

When his father arrived at the intended camp with his charges, Jon was not there. Irritated more than worried—A.K. knew his boy—he left the group setting up their tents and hiked on. He found Jon at the pack bridge camp, putting the finishing touches on his bribe: a pile of driftwood the size of a picnic table. It was with difficulty that A.K. convinced the child that the group would not be coming, no matter how pretty the camp, how entrancing the pack bridge, or how much wood had been gathered, and that it was Jon who would have to abandon his plan and rejoin the group.

By the time he was a young man, Jon Barker spent every possible moment on rivers, ridges and ski slopes. He graduated from high school one semester early, frustrated at rules that had prevented his leaving sooner. At 18 he began college but quit when he realized how many days of hunting, skiing and rafting that piece of paper would cost. He tried again a year later, this time planning to accomplish the goal by wedging semesters in where they did the least damage. That year he missed nearly every fall hunt and raft trip, as well as the entire first month of ski season. He dropped out again and never went back.

Uncompromising, self assured, and head over heels in love with rivers, Jon must have reminded Clancy of his own younger self. Like Jon, Clancy had once been certain that a life devoted to freedom and to making your living outside, to challenges like running with exacting grace the biggest whitewater you could find, was enough. It was enough even if a man couldn't articulate why, even if the world would never acknowledge that man's success, even if that man would spend his entire life poor in the eyes of the world. Clancy Reece had begun hinting to friends that he was growing less certain of those choices, but young Jon Barker must have been a fresh wind, his wild enthusiasms blowing dissatisfaction away.

Five

A Necessary Journey

*For seventeen years now, I've been a boatman. I take
people down whitewater rivers in the West. Through the
summer, I pretty much live on the river. Set up a kitchen at
a different camp each night, lay out a bedroll to sleep on the
river bank above the river running, below the stars shining.*

*I'm supposed to be there. I feel very much at home, at
ease and comforted, between the songs of the birds and water
and the silence of the stones and the canyon.*

*Still, when I went to put the boats in the water, I'd
look upstream at where I hadn't been. At the end of the trip,
I'd look back downstream and know it went to the sea. See?*

—Clancy Reece

F or years, Clancy had been telling friends that one day he'd
launch a raft into the Salmon River at the town of Salmon in

central Idaho and keep rowing for 770 miles until he hit the Pacific.

"Anything worth doing," he'd tell them, "is worth overdoing."

People got the impression he was hoping for takers, but the idea was nuts. The lower Columbia would comprise half the journey and that once fearsome river exists today as a chain of currentless reservoirs, each miles long and wide, each wind whipped, barge choked and, from a rafter's perspective, utterly unappealing.

Then the boy Jon Barker grew up and became a boatman, Clancy's kind of boatman: the kind who, when he's not working on rivers, floats them for fun and when he's not doing either, ponders them.

One summer not long after Clancy left his management job at Salmon River Challenge, he and Jon began talking, idly at first, about the journeys a person would have to complete before he could say he really knew a river. It quickly became clear to Clancy that the adventure that sounded pointless to his other friends, to Jon sounded necessary.

The two men decided they'd do it. They'd run the entire, freeflowing Salmon to its confluence with the Snake, keep rolling down the mostly conquered Snake to the Columbia, then float the completely conquered Columbia to the Pacific. They'd cross the entire Northwest entirely by river. Screw the ugliness and obstacles that the 20th century had managed to create from what had for thousands of years previous been a lovely, dangerous magic carpet ride.

Every foot of this river system had been traveled. Yet like history's most romantic expeditions, from the first North Pole expedition to the search for the headwaters of the Nile, a tracing of the entire system had almost certainly never been done. This was a first descent then, a first descent of the imagination if not of the map.

It was September, 1987. They would launch the following

June. Over the winter Jon would find a shuttle driver and obtain the gear. He'd gather the maps and learn whether the dams and locks on the lower Snake and Columbia, designed to facilitate commercial barge traffic, would allow small boats.

Clancy would build a dory. This dory would be able to navigate big whitewater of course, but that wasn't all. The men had agreed they would not use a motor even on the wide, currentless reservoirs. So when they reached that last 460 miles of dammed water, Clancy announced, this dory would *sail*.

One ancestor of the modern whitewater doryman was the Portuguese fisherman, known for his willingness to travel great ocean distances in his small craft. Portuguese dories looked odd to oarsmen from other parts of the world because their pilots faced in the direction of travel. That meant they pushed instead of pulling on their oars.

Early whitewater pioneers had faced their wooden boats opposite to the direction of travel. Their main rowing stroke was a downstream pull. The stroke is more powerful than a pushing stroke because it allows the whole body to contribute, but in whitewater it was problematic for two reasons. One was that a backward-facing oarsman could not as readily see approaching obstacles. The other was that the strong pulling stroke speeded the boat more quickly downstream, reducing planning and maneuvering time. The harder the oarsman rowed, the faster he closed the gap between himself and an obstacle.

As their sport matured, rafters and dorymen quickly adapted their crafts to the Portuguese style. Today, in flat water and especially against wind, they may spin their boats backward to take advantage of the more powerful pulling stroke, but in most whitewater they face forward, pushing on their oars to maneuver, or pulling backward to both maneuver and slow themselves in the current. Nodding to its history, a few whitewater boatmen still call their forward-facing downstream stroke a 'portagee.'

What Portuguese dorymen also did, when conditions were right, was step in a small mast and hoist sail.

Clancy was a student of boating history, so he probably knew about the Portuguese dorymen and their sails. Certainly as a green boatman working on the Colorado for a company called Grand Canyon Dories, he had watched experienced colleagues strap their spare oars so that the handles reached upward, then knot a plastic tarp between the 'masts.' They would sit back and, for as long as the wind cooperated, cruise.

But whitewater dories make ineffective sailboats. In big river canyons the prevailing daytime wind is brisk, but because it results from warm, rising air, it flows upcanyon. Dory boatmen could sail only on the rare days when the wind blew downcanyon, in the direction they wished to travel.

Real sailboats *can* travel upwind. They accomplish this not only by shaping their sails to act like an airplane's wing, but also by the V-shape of their hulls, by their keels which extend deep into the water, and by the rudders affixed to their sterns, all of which allow the force created by wind and sail to be converted into forward motion. Whitewater dories on the other hand need to be maneuverable, so they are nearly flat-bottomed and have no rudders. A dory spins at a single push-pull on the oars, but it will not sail upwind.

The boat Clancy envisioned would. It would have a real rudder, one that could be removed in whitewater. It would need a removable keelboard too. The hull would need at least a slight V-shape, which meant that this sailing dory would never turn as fast as a flat-hulled dory could. Clancy, confident of his strength, wasn't concerned.

Clancy's journals from that winter are scattered with sketches of boats. They are not blueprints. They look like a child's daydreamed escape vehicle. Clancy had little money and less boatbuilding experience, but his characteristic straight line approach to problem solving ignored those obstacles. That spring Clancy built the sailing whitewater dory which became part of his legend and which would be remembered by some as a rough and awkward craft and by others as a thing of genius.

Here is the description I found among those childlike drawings:

> I took a sailboat I had already. It was practically given to me by Captain Seaweed in Hurricane, Utah, back in '77, I believe. Like me, Captain Seaweed was a boatman and not fit for polite society. The boat he gave me was a 16 foot plywood, hard chine, centerboard V bottom trailer sailor with a Snipe rig. I gave some seriously foolish thought to doing the trip with that boat. Glad I didn't.
>
> I used it, though, for the foundation of the boat I did build. … I turned the sailboat upside down, and fastened batten to chines and to the bottom. … I cut wedge shaped pieces to fasten to the sides, to give a shape with more flare. I let the battens run past the stern of the sailboat for a longer boat.
>
> Drywall screws were used to tack everything together. A word on drywall screws: Those are the best thing since rock&roll. They are faster than nails, and you can re-use them. You don't have to pre-drill, you drive them in with a bit in a variable speed electric drill. After they hold pieces in place long enough for the epoxied glass tabs to set up, you set the drill to reverse and pull the things back out, leaving a hull with no metal in it.
>
> … The battens were skinned with 1/4 inch Doug fir

plywood, tacked in place with drywall screws. Glass tabs were epoxied on, allowed to set up, the screws were backed out, and the seams were sealed with glass tape & epoxy. Similar to [the] stitch & glue method, this is more like the screwed, glued, and canoed method. …

The sides were made 24 inches high, coincidentally half a sheet of plywood. The bottom got slathered with epoxy & covered with another layer of preslathered 1/4 inch Doug fir ply, held in place with the famous drywall screws. The screws were put in at 8 inch spacing starting at the center & working toward the ends, kinda sorta like torqueing the head on a motor. After the epoxy sets, the screws are pulled back out to be used again elsewhere.

The shell, or hull, was then pulled off the sailboat, or form, and turned over so the decks & hatches could be installed. This took a lot of sitting and looking and reaching to see that things were put where they would fit, and that things fit where they were put. Cogitate ergonomics, I thought; therefor I fit.

The open hull was decked over, and a footwell was placed in the approximate center with a slot along the left side to allow the footwell to be self-bailing, and to allow placement of a swing keel made of 1/4 inch steel plate. This meant my centerboard was a little left of center. That seemed appropriate. I'm a little left of center myself.

The side hatches were made as big as possible, to facilitate unloading and loading. … The bowpost & oarlock blocks were made of apricot wood, gotten out of a limb off a tree that grew by my house. The tiller came from a black locust down the street. A local junkyard yielded a sheet of aluminum for a rudder, scraps of stainless steel for brackets, & straps.

My buddy Jeffrey came up with stainless hinges from some war junk. My buddy Roger came up with strips of clear red fir from a remodeled building. He also brought good advice for a strong, sound & seaworthy boat. Ron Thompson brought a carpenter's skill, an artist's eye, and a bottle of tequila. Thank you, Ron, Roger & Jeff. Neither the boat nor I would have been as good or done as well without your help.

Six

Source to Sea: Launch

June, 1988

... The idea here: ride the flow of the river from a little brook in a Rocky Mountain meadow, where beaver dams and barb wire fences can span the flow and stand against the high waters of spring, all the way to the big salty.

As far as I know, no one has ever done this. Big deal. I haven't done this. That matters.

—Clancy Reece

Jon Barker found the video cassette at his parents' house. Its spine carries the year 1988, which was the year Clancy finished building his sailing dory and set out with his friend on a voyage that was supposed to be both a celebration of wild rivers and a rejection of the controlled state of modern rivers.

A year after beginning work on this book, I am back in Jon's old farmhouse to ask if they accomplished what they hoped to with that long voyage. Jon doesn't recall anyone filming their expedition, but he knows that's not the sort of thing he *would* remember. We slip the tape into his ancient VCR.

Bingo. On Jon's tiny television screen appears a narrow-torsoed young man. He is tangle-haired, boy-faced, nearly vibrating with excitement: Jon at 25. Beside him is Clarence 'Clancy' Reece. It's the first image I have seen of these two together and I am surprised. I suppose I had expected something father-and-son-like. After all, in this video Clancy is 43, 18 years Jon's senior. Nine-year-old Jon first experienced whitewater in rafts piloted by Clancy. As an adult, Jon's head barely tops Clancy's shoulder. The older man's bicep is as thick as the younger man's thigh. And yet despite age and size differences, what I see in their mock solemn posturing are two happy boys, complicit in a plot to enjoy this day beyond all reason.

They pose stiff and still-faced, in accidental resemblance to that Grant Wood painting, *American Gothic*, the farm couple's single pitchfork transformed into two double-bladed paddles.

"Anything—worth—doing—is—worth—overdoing," they chant.

At the first word Jon loses the battle, his grin spreading. Clancy remains solemn until the last, then allows a small smile to grow under his mustache. The smile is for the cameraman, their shuttle driver, and seems to say that Clancy is too self-aware to take even his own hijinks seriously.

Jon opens a palm in the direction of the river, talkshow host style, as though to introduce his special guest, the Salmon. The camera follows his hand. Here near the headwaters what it records is not a relentless river but a pretty stream. Shallow water polishes the tan cobble. Whip-twigged willows line the banks, still leafless although it is early June and summer has certainly arrived at lower elevations. Out on the valley floor a few brave wildflowers rise among last year's bunch grasses and winter-seared sage.

The dory Clancy built over the winter would be far too large for this tiny creek. It will wait on its trailer until the men reach the broader, deeper river downstream. Instead at each man's feet lies an 11-foot-long, one-person inflatable kayak. Boaters call them, for obvious reason, IKs, or, less obviously, duckies. The second nickname comes from the fact that, on commercial trips, guests who paddle the little IKs are constantly enjoined to "follow your mama," which is to say, the raft or kayak whose job it is to lead these novice paddlers safely through the rapids. The resulting parade looks like a duck and her ducklings. These particular duckies are red and blue Riken Cherokees. All that keeps them from looking like kids' pool toys are their sharply pointed sterns and bows and their businesslike rigidity.

In the video, Jon hauls his duckie forward so the nose dips into fast water. The stern remains awkwardly perched on the steep bank, forcing the duckie to tilt like a playground slide. Laughing, the young man straddles the craft from behind, then attempts to simultaneously shove the stern into the water and hop into the seat. He succeeds in the first, fails in the second and lands sprawled across the rear compartment. The duckie bucks, almost capsizing. Jon scrambles forward just in time to be swept, still laughing, into a twiggy curtain near the first corner.

Clancy, meanwhile, has pushed his duckie off the bank with his right leg and, with that same leg, pins the little craft to shore as he watches Jon's unceremonious entry. Then he steps aboard, takes two low, duckwalking steps forward on the unstable little boat's floor and folds his big body into paddling position. Quick backward strokes keep him from piling into his entangled friend.

"See what I mean?" says the middle-aged Jon Barker next to me, leaning intently into the blue light from his television. I assume he means Clancy's grace, how incongruous it appears in such a tree trunk of a man.

The camera watches as the younger man untangles himself and begins to disappear around the curve. Clancy backpaddles a few more times, then he too disappears and there is only the busy hiss and rush of the stream.

I glance at the stocky little man beside me. We're sitting on the matted shag carpet of an underfurnished living room in the gently aging farmhouse the young man in the video, who owned almost nothing, would have had no use for. High on the long list of things that young man did not need was a home. What he had were big dreams and a young person's seeming eternity in which to accomplish them. And friends, although I think that for the young Jon and even more for the one beside me, dreams and goals matter more than anything, including friendship. But they are tied together because Jon's goals can't be accomplished alone.

Does it hurt to watch this? I wonder.

But Jon is smiling. As he rewinds to watch their respective launches again he laughs out loud, unembarrassed at his near-dunking in an inches-deep stream, pleased with his friend's grace.

The camera shuts off.

The adventure that began with that launch lasted a month, far longer than planned. The river would test these two before it was done with them, test their courage and ingenuity but most of all their resolve. And in the end it would let them pass, and they would row out through the miles-wide, violently surging mouth of the Columbia, 912 miles downstream of their starting point.

It was a quixotic adventure, an undertaking many might admire but few would think to begin and far fewer would care to complete. You could imagine it featured in *National Geographic*, this expedition that traces the lower forty-eight's last big free river from its source. In fact, in 1935 a similar trip *was* a *National Geographic*-sponsored expedition. That earlier voyage had not used whitewater rafts or dories. Those did not exist in 1935. It used the craft which was then standard on the river, the wooden scow or sweepboat, so named for the 25-foot-long fore and aft arms that allowed the pilot to steer. The *National Geographic* expedition had begun at the town of Salmon, 145 miles downriver of Clancy and Jon's streamlike put-in. It had ended in Lewiston on Idaho's western border, 465 miles shy of the sea.

Fifty-three years separates these two voyages and yet during that time the Salmon River has changed little. It has been protected first by central Idaho's mountainous terrain and more recently by legislation. Below Lewiston, on the Snake and Columbia, that same timespan has changed everything. Had that *National Geographic* scow chosen to continue its journey rather than end at Lewiston, it could have ridden powerful river currents clear to the ocean. In 1988 when Clancy Reece and Jon Barker launched, those currents no longer existed. Instead eight dams made continuous slackwater reservoirs out of what had been, in 1935, two rivers even more powerful than the Salmon.

Seven

Headwaters to Salmon, Idaho

C lancy Reece had always intended to begin his seaward journey at the town of Salmon. He liked the nod to the daring sweepboat captains who had launched there back when this river, despite its challenges, was the most efficient supply route to mountain-locked central and western Idaho. The 1935 *National Geographic* expedition had also followed the sweepboats' lead and launched at the town of Salmon. In honor of that colorful, larger-than-life history, Clancy had for years called his dream adventure, 'Salmon to the Sea.'

But young Jon Barker had different ideas. Sure, he argued, from a historical standpoint a Salmon City launch made sense, but it didn't make river sense. If part of the idea was to trace the transformations of a river, the first five runnable miles were more important than any 50 further down. In those early miles, the Salmon changed from a trickle into a small river. No subsequent change was so dramatic.

Even if they started far above the town of Salmon, as high on the tiny stream as a duckie could float, the Salmon River really began at least another seven miles back. In fact, the true headwaters of the Salmon are a scribble of tiny, unrunnable springs trickling down mountain flanks. These trickles join like fingers to an arm on the alpine floor of the Sawtooth Valley. There at that wrist, at the first navigable water, argued Jon, was the lowest their journey could begin.

Won over, Clancy coined a new name, 'Source to Sea.'

Which was why, that first day, they found themselves scooting down a creek so narrow, and with bankside willows so dense, that sometimes they had to lie back and use their paddles to pry the red and tan twigs upward, creating tunnels to haul themselves through. Jon wished he'd brought ski goggles.

Four times the stream pooled behind beaver dams. Twice, enough water ran over the stick and mud walls that they were able to paddle up onto the dam until the boats' noses tipped out over empty space. They'd reach forward with their hands, hump up on top and teeter-slide down the back. Twice, though, the dams were higher, and they had to paddle up sideways, crawl precariously from the duckies to the top of the dam and climb over the ragged stick structures, dragging the little boats behind.

Which was fine, they told each other. Exactly as it should be, in fact. Anything worth doing ...

To their left, mostly hidden by greening streambank riot, rose the sheer, ragged Sawtooths, still holding the snowfields that would slowly become river over the course of the summer. The peaks made a torn edge for the blue sky as all that day the two paddled on a stream which became more riverlike with each tributary it swallowed.

They ran out of daylight, rolled out to sleep, got up in the morning and paddled to the mouth of Valley Creek and the tiny mountain town of Stanley, where their shuttle driver—and the dory—waited.

None of this is captured on the video. Jon relates all of it with the image of that tiny, willow-choked stream frozen on his television screen. Then he hits the play button and a new image appears. Jon tells me this must have been recorded the next morning. The fat cumulus clouds of the previous video image are gone. The sky is a rich, bottomless blue. I lean forward when I realize what I'm looking at. It's Clancy's famous boat.

Her white hull projects a bright reverse of herself onto the water on which she rides. She is tethered to a sloping bank just flushing green with new growth. The river in the background is now 50 feet wide but still has the dancing swiftness of a mountain stream. It's a scene so pretty it could have been staged for a big screen picture—white boat, glossy water, cobalt sky.

That day, the dory made its virgin whitewater runs. These *are* on the video. Before the boat arrives, the camera pans methodically across the first rapid. It is shallow and rocky. The dory drifts into view above the rapid. Clancy is standing at the oars for a better view, staring intently—rocks and wooden dories don't mix. In the bow Jon stands too but he's clowning, leaning back on the bowline like a waterskier. Apparently satisfied, Clancy sits and angles into a tongue of open water that extends partway into the rapid. He runs that tongue but gets funneled too close to the rock-studded left bank. He uses a foaming pillow of water upstream of a submerged rock to surf the dory back toward river center. It's a nice move but not quite enough, and the left side of the boat rides up on an exposed boulder. The dory lurches. At the bottom of the rapid Clancy turns to stare back upstream. His face is expressionless but I can almost read his mind. New boat or not, he's better than that. That won't happen again.

It doesn't. The second and third sets of rapids are on the video, too. The second is big and forceful, but Clancy dances the boat from one strand of current to another, from left bank to right to left, between holes and boulders. The moves require strength but the man's erect posture betrays little effort.

The third rapid is called Sunbeam. The rapid was created in 1934 when the only dam ever built on the Salmon was inexpertly dynamited by a Fish and Game contractor. Or at least that's the most likely version. Others include details like unmanned rafts loaded with explosives, pushed into the river above the dam by anonymous sportsmen. Either way, the idea was to allow any sockeye and chinook salmon that had survived the 20-year blockage to ascend to their ancient spawning grounds in the mountain lakes above. It's not yet clear even today whether the dam breach came too late for the salmon. Heroic attempts to save the tiny remnant handful of natural Sawtooth salmon began in 1999. But the explosion did eventually clear the way for something 1930s Sawtooth Valley residents would never have predicted, recreational whitewater rafting.

Some say Sunbeam, the rapid created by the remains of the dam, is the most interesting whitewater on the class III 'Piece of Cake' run. In the video Clancy finesses it.

Jon is pleased—and a little surprised—that he remembers where they camped that night, in a grassy pasture that ran like a green ribbon along the cottonwood-lined river. In his memory the camp is idyllic.

They rose the next morning aimed at the town of Salmon, the small farming and ranching seat of Lemhi County, home to some 7,000 people and 70,000 head of cattle. Salmon is isolated by central Idaho's crumpled topography and split in half by the river from which the town takes its name. Throughout the late 19th and early

20th centuries, the town's claim to fame was that it was the jumping-off point for those great wooden supply scows headed down the river through Idaho's rugged interior. Back then, the Salmon River had deserved the ominous-sounding nickname it still wears, 'River of No Return.'

The nickname was not coined as a warning. It articulated a simple fact: The cost effective way to run supplies down that river was for each scow to make a single journey. The scows, constructed in Salmon, typically measured 35 feet in length and eight feet in width. They ran loaded with trade supplies and even the occasional daring tourist. After they supplied miners and hermits along the river, as well as settlers in the west Idaho towns of Riggins, Whitebird and Lewiston, each scow was dismantled for its lumber. The pilots returned overland for the next journey.

These days Salmon is the staging spot for hundreds of Salmon River float trips every year. The rapids that were once navigational hazards have become the main attraction. The wilderness those scow pilots were trying to get through is what these new river travelers want to savor.

That night Clancy brought out the spiral binder in which he would write for the rest of the trip and which would, years later, be placed by his brother into my hands. It's mostly through Clancy's journal that I know that the trip which began so idyllically did not end that way. Jon, my other primary source, has a way of forgetting irrelevant details like risk, or how hard he had to work to achieve a goal. Those irrelevances lay weeks downstream, though. What Clancy wrote on the first page of his notebook was this:

> *We saw a young girl standing at the side of the river as*
> *we floated into Salmon. She didn't see us. We could both see*
> *she was going to be startled if we weren't gentlemen enough*

to announce our presence.

She was looking across the river and downstream. The only sound came from the water riffling over the cobble rocks of the bottom and some cars motoring across the bridge overhead.

The current carried us closer. Jon may have been holding his breath. I was. She knew she was totally alone, relaxing in a moment of safe solitude. What a pair of jerks!

We were about 15 feet away from her when I said HI!

The trick here is to time your howdy to the same instant you come into their peripheral vision. Soon as she got both feet on the ground at the same time, she gave us a really nasty look. We deserved worse.

We went to shore and tied up to a maple tree a hundred feet downstream. Upstream, we could see where the girl had been standing. She was gone.

We walked up into Salmon and to a restaurant where we ate greasy enormous double cheeseburgers, fries, coffee with cream, a side of french toast each, pie and vanilla ice cream.

I figure that's how Jim Bridger woulda done it.

Slept on the boat for the first time. One on each side hatch and a cooler on Jon's side, we leveled right out and had utterly comfortable accommodations. A few moments there, I sit up and look around. The river is running by, and the boat rocks a bit in the compression chop from the riffle that runs just there. The water must be warmer than the air, for foggy air haloes all the electric lights and drops a silver, softer light on everything else.

The river runs by and the boat rocks in the eddy. My boat. I built her myself from pieces and dreams. I'm glad she's so pretty.

Jon is asleep. A car motors across the bridge upstream. I remember the girl and smile. The river runs by and the boat rocks in the eddy.

God, I feel great.

Eight

North Fork, Idaho to Asotin, Washington

*Next morning happened right away and Barker was
chompin at the bit and overeager to be gone already. A quick
pull down to North Fork and breakfast.*

—Clancy Reece

At the small café, gas station and store named North Fork,
the Salmon makes an abrupt westward turn, aiming for
the first time at the eventual goal of all Northwestern water, the
Pacific. Nearly at the apex of that turn, the stream which lends the
store its name pours in, augmenting a flow that has already become
substantial.

Shortly after North Fork, the riverbank cottonwoods phase

out, their friendly pale green gradually replaced by the dark foliage and massive trunks of drought-resistant Ponderosa pines and Douglas firs. Except at water's edge, the willows disappear as well, as do the grassy banks and the river's playful tendency to braid itself about small islands of debris. Canyon walls rise up. The riverbed steepens, deepens, and the water that meandered aimlessly along the earth's surface now begins to bore into it in earnest.

This is the River of No Return about which stories are told and movies made, and against which boaters love to test themselves.

Jon had turned that North Fork corner several times in his young life. It made him feel small. He figured that was the point of big water: It let you feel your insignificance among earth-molding forces, but also reminded you that, small as you are, you could grab hold and ride, and that although you never controlled the river, you *could* control your ride.

The river's voice had changed as well. Now the calm stretches bespoke a deep expectant silence. Pools were interspersed not with riffles but actual rapids, where the river suddenly dropped in its bed or centrifuged around a curve, and then, lifting itself into arching waves, began to roar.

Boaters call this reach the Main Salmon or simply the Main. It passes through a vast roadless area which, including the Gospel Hump and Frank Church-River of No Return wildernesses, totals 3.3 million acres. Add the Selway-Bitterroot Wilderness (a single dirt road separates them) and you have a complex of wild, mountainous land larger than the state of New Jersey.

The Salmon carves its more-than-a-mile-deep gorge straight through not only the lower 48's largest remaining wilderness complex but also through the state's most prominent geologic feature, the Idaho Batholith, an island-sized mass of granite which forced its way up from inside the earth perhaps as recently as 45 million years ago and which comprises the crystalline core of the state.

It was one of those big sky, early summer days that seems to whisper in your sunburned ear that of course it will never end. The two men ran a score of class II and larger class III rapids. At midday they passed the mouth of the Middle Fork, the Main's largest tributary and a famous multi-day whitewater run in its own right. Eight miles beyond, the Salmon's gradient increased and the power of all that additional water made itself felt.

Here the dory got its first real test. The Main's first big rapids, Hancock, Split Rock, Big Mallard and Elkhorn, all have holes, waves or rocks big enough to capsize or flip a poorly handled boat. On a one boat trip, a flip could easily devolve into disaster. Who rescues the swimmers when everyone is swimming?

But one by one these rapids went off without a hitch. So did a dozen smaller rapids. The men declared the dory a success. It rocked onto its stern to climb each big wave. It sliced through the foaming top, sped down the back and climbed again, turning at light oar pressure to meet each crest straight and true, as a dory must. The men spun the boat this way and that, ferried across currents, rode the big waves, grinned at one another.

Or so Jon recalls, although truthfully this dory, with its modified sailing hull, should not have handled whitewater so well.

They also tried out the sailing keel although the experiment lasted only moments. Jon dropped the keel into its slot, Clancy turned the dory sideways to maneuver, and current caught the steel tongue now extending beneath the hull. The upstream gunwale dipped swiftly to the river's surface. Jon dove for the keel and hauled it back up. The boat settled flat in the water as though it had not nearly capsized a moment before.

Early evening found them at a long, low bench camp called Rhett Creek. They'd navigated nearly all the significant whitewater of the Main, running most of what is usually considered a weeklong trip in that one long day. They agreed that the dory had handled beautifully.

Ten miles ahead, the last major tributary to the Main, the South Fork, would meet the mainstem. Twenty-one miles past that they would run Chittam, the Main's last major rapid. Just below Chittam, the Salmon River Road appears on river left, by convention marking the end of the wilderness Main.

"Hey Twerp, what's the furthest you've ever rowed in a day?" asked Jon.

Clancy couldn't remember.

"Think you've gone a hundred miles?"

"Never," said Clancy.

Jon had rowed 100-mile days once or twice and been captivated by the idea. Not that any magic resided in the number 100. What he loved was that rowing a hundred river miles in a single day is impossible on most rivers. With few exceptions, the rivers of the world are either dammed, too slow-moving, too low-volume or too short. Most rivers with a youthful streambed and enough flow to host big whitewater give up their gradient in a few dozen violent miles and then lapse into flat-land calm. Or their waters were collected long ago behind dams, to be milked for electricity and dribbled out for irrigation.

It happens that if you hunt for 100 miles of navigable whitewater that can feasibly be run in a single day, you'll find yourself looking mostly at a handful of rivers in the mountainous state of Idaho. Through an accident of geology, several Idaho rivers lose elevation steadily, in the Salmon's case at a respectable 10 to 14 feet per mile over most of its 409 mile length. But even on those few rivers a 100 mile day is possible only if you plan well. A whitewater dory gets something like four-fifths of her speed from current and one-fifth from the oarsman. Idaho's biggest rivers provide the current speed necessary to travel a 100 miles in a single day only during spring runoff.

Most of Jon's friends didn't get his 100 mile thing. Why work that hard? they asked him. So perhaps Jon was expecting to be teased yet again when, one hand full of maps, he told Clancy they had rowed 100 miles that very day. One hundred and five, in fact. But the big man's eyes went lively with interest. As usual when it had to do with rivers, Clancy got it.

"Makes you wonder what we could do if we *tried*," he deadpanned.

They rowed out of the wilderness the next morning, watching the Salmon's final transformation. Over a dozen or more miles, the forested slopes and sheer granite walls faded into sage and bunchgrass hills. Through those tan slopes, like black bones through flesh, thrust basalt buttresses footed with crumbling black basalt blocks. Stands of pine became mountain mahogany and the occasional monolithic ponderosa. Suddenly the men were no longer on a forested mountain river: The Salmon now carved its dramatic canyon through desert.

They reached Riggins at midday. Barely more than one street wide, no part of town is more than a stone's throw from the river upon which it depends. The two clambered up the steep bank for a burger and to find out if the Salmon River would allow them to continue.

It would not.

Thirty-three miles from Riggins, the Salmon enters a second remote section, 53 miles of close basalt gorges alternating with sky-filled, open reaches. In the middle of the fourth and most dramatic gorge, a tumbled mass of raw stone extends from the left wall. By coincidence, it narrows the river exactly where the canyon pinches in from the right as well. The rapid that results exists only at high and moderate water levels. It's called the Slide.

Bureau of Land Management records say that the rapid was formed in 1950 by a natural landslide. The cliff wall fractured and sent 170,000 cubic yards of rock crashing into the river's path, briefly blocking the entire flow. At the time, the area was wilderness in the old sense—not a physically embattled albeit legally protected preserve, but a remote and economically trivial place, and therefore an undisturbed one. So although a rancher up Flynn Creek reported feeling the ground shake, no official report of the event was filed until 1956, when a regional Fish and Wildlife Service director rode in on horseback to take a look at the blockage.

What he saw then was probably much like what you'd see at high flows today, a roaring madhouse.

Unlike most of the river's big rapids, this one is generated not by midstream boulders or sharp corners, but simply by a big river bulling through a slot better suited to a creek. At low flows the Slide consists of ripples and whisperings. It becomes forceful enough to be tricky at 17,000 cubic feet per second (cfs). It regularly flips boats at 20,000 cfs. Most consider it unrunnable above 30,000.

A decade earlier, Clancy had led a four-boat commercial trip down the Slide during spring runoff. In old reel-to-reel tape of that escapade, the rapid's top wave looks like a foaming, nearly river-wide mouth, yawning upstream.

Watching that film is an exercise in humility. First to float into the camera's view is a dory piloted by an experienced boatman named Barry Dow. He has told the other oarsmen that he plans to run left of that frightening mouth, so he enters the rapid sideways, pulling hard toward the left bank. But the water is moving faster than it appears and he hits the monster wave before he can straighten into it, all his effort having managed to keep him barely 10 feet left of its powerful center. The dory nearly capsizes, but then settles and swirls rightside up through the next waves, helpless as a leaf in a gutter. At the bottom of the rapid it nearly plows into a cliff wall, an error no doryman can stomach.

Clancy and the other two oarsmen watch, then decide to take their chances in the center. One by one as the camera watches, they hit that top wave and flip, as casually as if the Slide were a short order cook.

A jetboat waited just below the rapid to pick up pieces— Clancy's boss, Curt Chang, had feared trouble. Clancy and the other guides had too, so most of the guests had been left ashore to scramble past the rapid on the rocks. Those precautions transformed what could have been an ugly story into another bit of river lore.

But in 1988 Jon and Clancy had no backup. So they cooled their heels. They gave a newspaper interview, visited friends, watched time slip by. Each had guiding commitments he couldn't put off forever.

Almost a week later the water had finally dropped to 20,000 cfs. Only a bit behind schedule, the men set off again.

There is another video clip, filmed the day they left Riggins. In the image, the river is wide and brimming with sun, and the hills roll back to a sun-filled sky. The dory is tiny on that broad expanse of water, a pretty white toy. The day is warm and Jon is shirtless as he rows. Neither man wears a lifejacket. Clancy is casting his spinning rig off the stern, first toward the right and then the left, effortlessly, as another person might twiddle his thumbs.

It's the kind of Huck Finn moment those who cram outdoor recreational lives into weekends yearn for. These men are more than a week into their journey. Big rapids, including the Slide, and hundreds of miles stand between them and their goal, rendering time an abstraction. For each man, challenge, the river, and his companion comprise all that is significant.

That next afternoon, after a surprisingly unremarkable ride through the Slide, having run the entire Lower Salmon and its whitewater, usually a five-day trip, in little more than one long, hard day, they spilled out onto the even larger Snake.

The whitewater challenge was finished, the wilderness successfully navigated. But neither man had had any doubt about completing this first phase of their adventure. The questions and unknowns lay downstream. The real adventure was about to begin.

There were some 500 miles of river yet to trace. Neither man had ever negotiated a dam and they would encounter dam after dam. The dory had not yet proven itself on flatwater and ahead of them lay reservoir after reservoir. Instead of wilderness, they would find cities and factories along the shores, giant barges plying the waters between, and then, finally, the sea.

Seven miles above the town of Asotin, Washington, the two saw a gray-haired man dressed in jeans and cowboy boots. He stood on the bank, waving them in. They couldn't imagine what he wanted, but the unwritten law of the river says that if someone calls, you stop. Clancy rowed over.

As soon as they were within earshot, the old man cupped a hand to his mouth and hollered across the water, "Hey, you're the guys I read in the paper is going to the ocean, aren'cha?"

They glanced at one another. They had forgotten about the newspaper interview. They said they were.

"Best of luck, boys. Best of luck. Wish I was comin' along," yelled the old man. And he waved them happily on.

Nine

Riding the Wind

The final video clip of that 1988 Source to Sea voyage opens on Jon Barker in warm, late afternoon light. He stands on a dock coiling the dory's bowline. From his seat in the rowing compartment Clancy Reece stows gear. The dory's mast is stepped in, its keel and tiller down. Jon tells me the footage was shot at the Asotin Marina, a few miles above Lewiston on the Idaho/Washington border, which means the dory has not yet sailed but is about to.

They had arrived in Asotin the previous afternoon, Jon explains, and had gotten a ride into town to resupply. After a week's hard work on the oars, what the men hoped for was a 500 mile hitchhike on the wind.

The 1805 Lewis and Clark expedition, perhaps the first group of non-natives to navigate the Lower Snake and Columbia rivers and certainly the first to meticulously document what it saw, found roiling current and more than 100 rapids between what is now Lewiston, Idaho and the sea. As the storied Northwest Passage, which was supposed to open the Northwest the way the Mississippi had opened the central U.S., the Columbia, more restless leviathan than road, had been a disappointment.

Less than two centuries later, the lower Snake and Columbia rivers have been engineered into exactly the inland waterway Lewis and Clark had been sent to find. Only the final 90 miles of the Columbia, below the last dam, boasts noticeable current. Which meant that Clancy's sailing dory needed to work, or the men would be forced to row nearly 500 miles of lake, almost certainly into an upstream wind.

To mark the beginning of the sailing phase, Clancy had returned that afternoon with a mascot and, when Barker River Trips' shuttle driver Laurie Skow arrived with her two children to see the men off, Clancy had the kids duct tape his new passenger to the bow. Every sailing ship needed a masthead, he told them solemnly as they affixed the Barbie doll.

By the time the camera flicks on, Barbie is ready to ride and "the two little puke faces," as Jon called Laurie's boys to their perverse delight, are stepping off the dory. Clancy and Jon don't seem to notice. The silliness is out of the way. The obvious aim of every motion and clipped, quiet word is to get on the water.

The oars have been strapped to the boat's deck, so Clancy uses the newly attached tiller to scull out from shore. The boat wriggles from side to side like a happy dog. Once in deeper water, Clancy directs Jon to untie and raise first the main sail, then the jib. The main bellies immediately. The jib luffs and then fills as Clancy adjusts the tiller. And then the two whitewater boatmen are sailing away down the Snake.

The camera shuts off.

To Jon, that evening seemed magical. Clancy tacked back and forth, advancing on a series of 45 degree angles that add up to that counterintuitive calculus of sailing, where wind, sail and keel together push a boat in an impossible direction, upwind. Jon watched carefully. Their zig-zagging reminded him of chicken scratches, his name for the tracks alpine skiers leave when making the abrupt jump turns required on extreme slopes.

As they advanced, they passed through the river's final trans-formation. Just the day before, they had watched the West's two largest inland rivers, the Salmon and Snake, join and roll on as one. That combined momentum had seemed unstoppable, but of course it was not. Although still 20 miles downriver, Lower Granite Dam's influence reaches up to Lewiston, erasing the river's downstreaming. The men sailed into an arrested calm. Curb-high waves roughed the water's surface, but they were wind-driven, not current-built.

Jon and Clancy, both raised in Lewiston, didn't question the dams that made their town into an inland seaport. In the late 1980s dams and the logic which had led to their construction still seemed impregnable. Western politicians wouldn't begin to entertain argu-ments for restoring natural flow to Western rivers for another decade, even though the science in favor of dam removals had been stacking up long before the last of the West's big dams had been built.

On the other hand, both men could remember the old Snake River. Until 1975 when Lower Granite Dam was completed, current still rolled past Lewiston and, although their numbers were plum-meting, so did the remnants of massive salmon and steelhead runs that had been vital for Northwestern ecosystems, providing a living upstream transport system for minerals and meat. The runs had also been foundational for the region's human cultures and more recently the basis for booming commercial fisheries.

Clancy Reece often wished aloud to friends that the Snake River dams didn't exist. His reason was pure Clancy: It was in the order of things that he should be able to catch the same free ride that had once whisked salmon and steelhead smolts to the Pacific.

Also pure Clancy was the fact that, as a young man, he had worked as a powder monkey on the last of these dams. Whitewater boatmen are better known for their sour jokes about wishing they could blow up dams than for helping to build them, but Clancy relished such contradictions in his history. A ballet dancer and a boxer? Sure, why not? And why not a dam builder who became a lover of freeflowing rivers?

Jon tells me now that although they didn't discuss it, dam protest was the subtext of this trip. Not an attempt to change anything but a statement, mostly to themselves, that they were on the side of free rivers and anadromous fish, not that of cheap electricity, cheap barge transport or cheap irrigation.

The confluence of the Snake and Clearwater at Lewiston brought a moment the men had anticipated. Jon thought of it as turning the corner. When Clancy and Jon finished a Snake River commercial raft trip, they took out at a place called Heller Bar. They drove with the guests downriver to the confluence of the Snake and Clearwater and then turned right, up the Clearwater into Lewiston, while the water they'd been floating on bent west and headed for the Pacific without them.

This night, as dusk drew the canyon walls intimately near, Clancy made a long tack at the meeting of the Clearwater and Snake, and then that much-discussed seaward turn. This time, where the river went, so would they.

Jon celebrated the moment by sending his mind 96 miles up the Clearwater to the confluence of the Selway and Lochsa and then beyond, up the wilderness Selway past boulder-tumbled, unrunnable

Selway Falls, and finally into the treeless granite peaks of the Bitterroot Mountains, cupping their crystal lakes. He could feel the weight of all that land tipping toward this place, all that water slipping toward this moment. If he trailed his fingers over the side of the dory, he'd touch waters drained from Idaho, Utah, Wyoming, Washington, Oregon and Nevada. All those wild, windswept heights feeding this low, slow, conquered place. Jon said none of this to Clancy. He was positive he didn't have to.

The men sailed into darkness and two hours beyond. The dory's mastlight was a firefly spark among the green and red navigational lights marking the deepwater channel for the now ubiquitous barges.

They progressed only a little faster than if they'd been rowing. Had one of them strode briskly along shore, he'd almost keep up. This would take getting used to: In the currents upstream the men had been making upwards of 10 miles per hour.

Fifteen miles below Asotin they tied up to shoreline riprap and unrolled their sleeping bags on the deck, happy with the day behind them. They were less excited about the one ahead. They would wake on a vanquished river, ugly as a corpse.

But dawn surprised the men by illuminating a pretty canyon of crumbled basalt cliffs topped by grassy bluffs. A few dirt roads penetrated the canyon but they seemed infrequently traveled. Except for the lack of current and the gray 'bathtub lines' visible on shoreline rocks at the reservoir's most typical levels, the men might have believed themselves still on a wild river.

Lower Granite Dam appeared at midday, first as a gray line drawn upon the water. As they drew nearer, the line became a concrete curb. Dwarfed by the canyon, it appeared almost low enough to step onto, nowhere near substantial enough to hold back most of the Northwest's water. Beyond it was nothing but sky.

Up close, the 'curb' finally revealed itself as a concrete wall thick enough at its tapered top to drive a truck across. A long, narrow structure ran crosswise to the graceful curve. This was the lock.

The men learned that day that, no matter how you felt about dams, passing through locks was incredible fun. As they would at each lock for the rest of their journey, they rowed up to a concrete jetty extending from the face of the dam and pulled on a fat rope to ring a bell. A voice crackled out of a speaker above their heads. They couldn't see the voice's owner although he seemed to see them. The voice directed them into the lock, which turned out to be a roofless hallway with a water floor.

Jon had called before the trip. He'd learned that as long as a craft was large enough to handle the turbulence generated by lock operation, the operator would let that craft 'lock through.' That was part of the deal under which these dams had originally been approved. So although the locks were designed to accommodate 3,000 ton barges and their tugs, that massive machinery also ground into motion for whitewater dories weighing 300 pounds, carrying little besides two men who grinned with exhilaration and the feeling that they were getting away with something.

At each lock, as soon as the men moored to a float as the voice directed, the water inside the cavernous hallway began to drop. But that wasn't what appeared to happen. The wet walls seemed to grow upward at a rate of an inch or two per second. After twenty minutes, the dory floated at the bottom of an 85-foot-long, 60-foot-high bathtub. Giant doors swung out or rolled up, depending on the lock's design, and the men rowed out into the sun on what for a moment appeared to be, if enough turbines were running, a living river. Behind them the dam revealed itself not as a low wall but as a soaring concrete arc.

The two agreed that they'd never felt more like Huck Finns

than on these first days of flatwater travel. Dwarfed by the massive dams, by the big barges and the water's engineered stasis, the little dory sailed along. At each dam, an invisible someone said, "Move ahead," then lowered them to the waterway below. Two outlaws on a pole raft in a Mark Twain novel couldn't have had more fun.

Clear, calm June days stretched before and behind them. The Lower Snake canyon continued to be pretty. When there was enough wind to fill the sails, say 10 miles per hour or so, they sailed. Otherwise they rigged the oars and rowed. They made perhaps 30 miles each day, but only by starting at dawn and continuing until dark, mostly through Jon's prodding. Clancy humored his friend, some days more sourly than others. Goals were fine but they did not evaporate if you set them aside to enjoy a good night's sleep, a six-pack of cold beer, or a promising fishing eddy.

They talked about how they'd like to spend a season working the great barges. Passing through like this, they were party crashers. It would be another thing entirely to learn this water and the ways men made their livings from it. That was something guiding had taught them: When you make a thing your livelihood, you learn it in ways otherwise impossible.

The men locked through three more dams, Little Goose, Lower Monumental and Ice Harbor, one an almost magical occurrence because it took place at night.

That dam, Lower Monumental, first appeared not as a gray line but a span of bright dots in a black world. As the men approached, the dots became streetlights on arched posts. Beneath each post, a bright puddle reached toward them across the water's skin. It was incongruous, all that light shouting from an otherwise abiding darkness.

Entering the hallway was wonderfully strange. The black water seemed to suck them down and away from the lights atop the dam. When they were released from the lock, they moved from a close blackness into a huge, open blackness. Clancy turned the dory and pulled, rowing away on a spillway-generated current they could feel but not see.

They spent that night less than a mile upstream of the mouth of the Snake, tied to the dock at Sacagaweah Park. Like so many places along their route, including their hometown of Lewiston and its sister city, Clarkston, the park owes its name to Lewis and Clark's Corps of Discovery. Sacagaweah was a Shoshone woman who had traveled with Lewis and Clark. The explorers had camped at that spot in early October of 1805.

For several miles the canyon walls had been gradually lying back until, there at the park, the landscape was for the first time flat and open. Lewis and Clark had found it desolate, describing "open country where the eye has no rest." Jon and Clancy found it green as only irrigated desert can be, verdant with well-watered orchards, vineyards and fields of alfalfa.

The next morning they reached the mouth of the more than 1,000-mile-long Snake and sailed out onto the Columbia. A true behemoth among rivers, the Columbia's headwaters are in Canada, and its mouth 1,240 miles downstream on the Oregon/Washington coast. It's the largest river in the West, fourth largest in the country. It carries the waters of a Who's Who list of Western rivers, including the Lochsa, Selway, Salmon, Middle Fork, Payette, Owyhee, Snake, Deschutes, White Salmon, Blackfoot, Clearwater, Kootenay and Clark Fork. The dorymen left the Snake and the Snake came with them, and together they headed down the Columbia toward the sea.

Ten

Into the Teeth of the Wind

On October 16, 1805, men from Lewis and Clark's expedition paddled dugout canoes onto the Columbia, hopeful that they had found a national treasure.

Cartographers of the time were pretty sure the storied Northwest Passage existed. Thirteen years earlier, a Boston fur trader had noticed a huge freshwater outlet high on the Pacific Coast at what is now the Washington/Oregon border. He'd named it after his vessel, the Columbia Rediviva, and speculated that the Northwest Passage would have just such a massive mouth. Lewis and Clark believed that if there was a Northwest Passage ending at that outlet, this river was almost certainly it: Trappers' stories said this was the largest river in the region.

The Columbia would eventually prove to be that and more. It

was home to what may once have been the world's greatest salmon runs. The year Lewis and Clark encountered the Columbia, perhaps 16 million salmonids surged up the river to spawning grounds in Washington and Oregon and as far inland as Idaho, Wyoming and Nevada.

Lewis and Clark perceived this keystone event of Northwestern ecosystems as an almost incomprehensible waste. Unlike Atlantic salmonids, nearly all Pacific salmon die after spawning. The explorers encountered fish carcasses lying like cordwood along the banks, jostling each other by the hundreds, filling the air with their stench.

But Columbia River tribes relied heavily on the runs. That year, residents of the region probably harvested some 42 million pounds of valuable, reliable meat, much of it without the effort and risk involved in hunting. Tribes further inland benefited as well, since salmon flesh could be dried and traded. The runs were also a natural transport system, carrying nutrients from rich ocean waters to animals and riparian plants many hundreds of miles from the sea.

The Columbia is remarkable in other ways as well. Most of North America's big rivers only become massive as they reach their lowlands. By then they lack the gradient and restricted channel that makes rivers easy to harness for hydropower. The Mississippi, for instance, loses less than 100 feet of elevation from St. Louis to the Gulf of Mexico. That's a drop equalling the height of a Ponderosa pine, spread over 700 miles of river. The Columbia drops nearly twenty times as fast, falling more than a thousand feet in its last 400 miles alone.

Some 70 years ago that unique combination of drop and volume attracted the kind of attention rivers don't survive. Nearly all big modern rivers are dammed, but few as thoroughly as this one. Columbia River dams today produce power which is consumed all along the Western seaboard. Cities, irrigated farmlands, and water- and power-dependent manufacturing plants line the lower river's banks. Upstream and down roll the massive barges, loaded with grain and other goods. At its confluence with the Snake, the Columbia today is over a mile across, twice the width of the river Lewis and Clark encountered. Those massive salmon runs are a chapter in a history book.

Yet Jon Barker and Clancy Reece learned that even here their world consisted primarily of water, basalt bluff, and sky. Even when I-84, the region's biggest east-west highway, joined the river some 30 feet above their heads, it felt irrelevant to the men in the boat below. They had been traveling on water so long that only water mattered. The journey was an equation unto itself. The wider world had disappeared.

And there was this: Some of the water beneath the dory had meandered across the Sawtooth Valley, bored through the Idaho Batholith, and rolled north onto the Snake with them. That water did continue toward the sea, even if it did so with an imperceptible westward slouching, completing in torpid weeks a journey that had once taken days. Which, the men reminded each other, was why they were going.

If they had felt small on the Salmon and Snake, here they were ants. The reservoirs, dams, barges, and wind-lifted waves were all built to a scale that rendered the little dory a thing of insignificance.

The water was colder too, some 48 degrees, thanks to the deep reservoirs in which it was repeatedly held. The men agreed that in the unlikely event that the boat capsized and they had to swim for shore, hypothermia would incapacitate them long before they could reach safety. Of course, there was no reason why the boat should capsize. So although Jon carried his drysuit, waterproof with rubberized gaskets at neck, wrist and ankle, he didn't wear it on this flat water. Clancy called the things 'poopy suits.' He had never owned one. His protective gear was a trademark cheap rubber rainsuit, useful against spray and splash but no help at all if he swam.

Their second day on the Columbia the men had intended to sail through the night. Time was growing short and they had lost nearly a day making repairs to a cracked tiller. Near sundown the wind built to perhaps 25 miles per hour. In order to make way, they had to abandon the safety of near-shore water and begin making miles-long, river-wide tacks, heading first for the highway lights on the Oregon side, and then the more intermittent lights of a road on the Washington side. This put them, for the first time, directly among the barges.

Each 'tow' consists of a diesel-powered tugboat shoving a payload of up to five long, squat barges laced together with steel cables. The best way to picture these behemoths is to imagine a skyscraper lying on its side, being pushed along by the wailing engines of a tugboat at 10 miles per hour. The cables that hold the barges together are as thick as a child's arm. A full tow can measure 650 feet in length and haul 15,000 tons of cargo. Even against that night's fierce wind the tows made seven miles per hour, kicking spray 100 feet or more into the air as they crashed through the wind-lifted waves. Bright warning lights shone from their bows and powerful horns blasted loud enough to be heard clear across the river.

The men had other problems that night. Big waves hissed toward them every few moments. These were not stationary river waves. Boaters can slow their approach to river waves or even dodge them altogether. A boater who knows his river well knows where the dangerous waves will be because, although river waves morph in character and size with variations in water level, their locations don't change unless the river channel changes. Some river waves even have names, like Five-Oh or House Wave or Glass Wave.

But the Columbia's wind-built waves were not stationary.

They charged upriver like lines of infantry. Watery hills loomed occasionally out of the darkness, but even the smaller waves were big enough to capsize the dory if Clancy didn't swing to meet each one straight on. The wind blew heavy spray from each wave's crown into the men's faces, blinding Clancy just as he needed to react.

Another problem was that the wind was far too strong for the men to row against. In order to move upwind under sail, Clancy had to tack at a precise angle to the wind, turn out of his tack to take the big waves bow-first, then resume his tack as the dory fell down the wave's backside. Each time he turned to face a wave, he lost ground on his tack. Each time he delayed that turn until the last instant, he risked a flip.

The wind-whipped darkness provided no frame of reference. So although the men could tell from its bright lights when a barge was coming, they couldn't guess its angle or speed of travel until it was within perhaps half a mile, or five minutes' barge travel away. The men were averaging a half mile per hour downstream and could move a few hundred yards left or right in that same five minutes. This was barely more than the length of a tow.

The men were also nervously aware that their little firefly of a mastlight was probably invisible to the bargemen through the wind-whipped spray.

They might have been even more discomforted had they known how difficult tug pilots consider the Columbia when its famous winds rise. Steering a craft shaped like a city office building is not easy. Under optimal conditions, a loaded tow moving at full speed needs a quarter mile of calm water in which to stop. Add wind to the equation and the skyscraper gains a mind of its own. In windy conditions those massive cables can snap, scattering the tow. Because they sit high, empty barges must be tacked like sailboats. Every experienced Columbia tug pilot has hit something he didn't want to. Nearly always, the ultimate cause was wind.

After a few more nervewracking tacks across the barge channel, far riskier for Clancy in his slicker than Jon in his drysuit, Clancy aimed the dory at a sheltered cove. There they found a well-made dock, a yacht club maybe. They knew if they looked around, they'd probably find a No Trespassing sign as well, so they didn't look. Jon cinched them to a cleat and the exhausted men rolled out their bags and fell asleep.

The next day was calm, but they were nearing the top of the 100 mile Columbia Gorge, the windiest section of what may be the West's windiest river. They didn't expect the calm to last. They didn't want it to: As long as it wasn't as strong as the previous night, wind would allow them to sail.

The Gorge is the only near-sea-level channel through the coastal Cascades. The very different climates on either side of that mountainous wall, one moist and the other desert-dry, engage in a neverending attempt to balance each other through that gap. Jon and Clancy knew this, just as they knew that the Gorge was becoming a mecca for a new sport, windsurfing. 'Boardheads,' as they would be called in another decade, were not yet as ubiquitous as they would become, but already they were a mainstay for Gorge towns like Hood River, Oregon.

So sure, there would be wind. In the river canyons Clancy and Jon knew, strong convection winds blow upcanyon most summer afternoons, while mornings and nights tend to be calm. It seemed reasonable to expect the same pattern here, although perhaps stronger.

Ordinarily they would have been right, but when big storms roll off the Pacific and hit the Cascades, some of that force funnels into the only outlet available: the Columbia Gorge. When that happens, the upcanyon winds blow in earnest. As Jon and Clancy approached the Gorge and basalt canyon walls began again to rise, enclosing the river, just such a storm reached the Pacific coast.

The wind stirred. Then it blew. And blew. Thirty miles per hour, 40, 50. For one implacable, impossible week. Every day and all night, day after day.

Just like that, the game was no longer a game, and a mile was no longer something that passed unremarked every fifteen or thirty minutes. It was a goal the men sweated for foot by foot.

Sailing, they gained ground only painfully. They slammed through big wind-blown waves, one man highsiding to keep the boat upright and the other steering, both men soaked and half-blinded by spray, each moment bringing the possibility of a capsize. Their tacks were mile-wide, hour-long jogs that bought, at best, a few hundred feet of downstream progress.

Rowing, their progress was less abysmal, but each stroke took a man's full strength and moved the dory downstream a foot or two if they were in the partial shelter of a shoreline cove, six inches if they were exposed to the full brunt of the wind. Clancy rigged something he called a drogue or drag, an underwater 'sail' that ran off the front of the dory to catch current—when there was any.

Breaking back out of those coves into the teeth of the wind was as hard as anything Jon had ever done. He'd wrench so hard on the oars that his body would rise from the seat, every muscle rigid. Then, if he didn't complete the stroke by immediately throwing forward to start another, he'd lose whatever tiny gain he'd achieved.

Those howling days, the men learned to count themselves lucky if they made ten miles in twelve hours of struggle and risk. The hundred mile day on the Salmon, even those thirty and forty mile days on the Lower Snake, seemed as though they had never happened.

On the worst day they managed less than three miles and that only by dogged—and to Clancy's mind ridiculous—will. That day they attempted to sail, then to row, with and without the help of the drogue. They rapidly decided rowing was impossible and again hoisted sail. But the wind roared even harder than on previous days; on some of their tacks they made no progress at all.

Clancy wanted to quit for the day, but Jon wouldn't hear of it. What if the wind never stopped? For the first time, the possibility arose that they would not finish—and was summarily dismissed. Their guiding jobs would start in a couple weeks and a man had to eat. But quitting this far along was unthinkable. Wind or no wind, they would finish. In time. Somehow.

Sitting in Jon Barker's farmhouse all these years later, I ask whether they discussed throwing a motor on the back of the dory, just until the wind died down. Jon looks at me in displeased surprise and makes no other comment.

That day on the Columbia, Jon finally even climbed out onto the wind-whipped shore, wrapped a line half-around his torso and, with Clancy feathering an oar on the offside to keep the boat off the rocky bank, bent almost double into the rope. For as long as his strength lasted, Jon dragged his friend's dory toward the Pacific.

Each time they stopped that week, they had to search out a safe landing. They looked for protected coves, beaches, anything but the ubiquitous 'riprap,' the stabilized jumbles of sharp boulders that are characteristic of an engineered waterway. They took advantage of swimming beaches and docks both public and private. One man always slept onboard, no matter how much the boat surged in the swell and how little he therefore slept, in case the dory broke loose.

Clancy's spiralbound journal has a lot to say about that week. When he was alive, Clancy never offered to show Jon what he wrote about their trips and Jon, for whom the sight of his friend scribbling was simply part of life, never asked. Looking backward was not something the young Jon was inclined to do, not when the next adventure lay in another direction.

I have brought the journal from this trip so I can show it to Jon. He reads his friend's words aloud, repeats phrases he likes. He reads one section complimentary to himself, says wonderingly, "Wow. That's cool he thought that," and then asks to copy the whole notebook.

6/21/88

Jon and I have been developing new skills at highsiding. The combination of strong, erratic wind, upstream rollers, downstream current, and both ways barge traffic would have kept boredom away even without the stabbing when we went to fix the broken rudder.

The locust limb started developing cracks and creaks and twisting when I tried to steer with it. We pulled into beautiful waterfront Wallula Junction, where Jon called Steve Hoffman, a friend of his who farms near Eureka, Washington. We took the rudder to his shop, [repaired it,] and headed back to the boat.

A call on the C.B. told Steve, who is part of the E.M.S. service ... to respond to a call in Eureka. Those guys have got their stuff together. We weren't five miles away when the call came out & we were the third rig to the scene.

A Mexican guy whose name was not Umberto was lying on the porch, looking depressed. I don't blame him. His guts were hanging out. A gauze compress on top and quite a lot of adhesive tape around the area stuck him back together for the ride into the hospital. A M.A.S.T. unit (Military Anti Shock Trousers) was fitted on him but not inflated, in case he got more shocky. His neighbors were talking in Spanish & I heard the name "Umberto" time and again. A pot-bellied sheriff's deputy showed up & asked the stabbee the name of the stabber. He said "Manuel Gonzales" and nobody said any different.

I personally suspect that "Manuel Gonzales" is the ethnic equivalent of "John Doe," "Jim Jones," or "Chuck Smith."

Once the victim was given the standard EMT "treat for shock, immobilize and transport," we took us & the rudder back to beautiful Wallula to resume our trip.

We had expected to sail through the night to make up for time lost fixing the rudder, but the aforementioned combination of wind, rollers, darkness and military-spec diesel driven fog horns from the barges persuaded me to prove I'm a wimp by seeking shelter.

Next day there was no wind so we rowed. We could see some electric power towers downstream when we started rowing. [At the end of the day] we could still see those damn electric towers [although now they were behind.]

We wanted wind so we didn't have to row. We got wind. And waves. Sailing into weather, the boat develops enough momentum to ride up over those waves, then the bow of the boat lands splat flat on the next wave, killing momentum, and causing the boat to side slip. I figure we're sailing six miles back & forth to make one mile down.

We're holed up in Arlington now, waiting for the wind to die down.

So we can row.

6/23/88

 Rusty's T-Bone Café
 Beautiful downtown Rufus, Oregon

Drinking coffee and waiting for the wind to slow.

It was just getting light this morning when Barker got on the boat where I was sleeping on the deck. The wind was blowing maybe 20 miles per hour, rollers two feet plus, & Barker was worried we'd miss some time for getting down the river. I was warm & dry & fully content to let the wind just keep on blowing & rocking me.

"This is foolish," I said.

"We'll never know if we don't try," he said.

So we tried.

It was foolish.

Now we know. One hour's hard work by Jon at the sticks got us maybe 200 yards downstream. Bullshit. We let the wind blow us back up the river & to the dock. Tied up.

Barker's back sleeping in the park. I'm hanging out, bored, in Rufus. That's what you do in Rufus.

Maryé Barker & Laurie Skow came down with food yesterday & went through locks with us. Below the dam, the wind started just whipping. Waves got three foot plus.

We got the main up & down in a scene of flogging confusion. The ladies seemed serene & confident. The look on Jon's face said he was as concerned as I was. I didn't like it out there.

After I first read this entry in Clancy's journal, I called Laurie Skow to ask how she and Jon's mom, Maryé, ended up running the locks at John Day Dam, and what Clancy meant by "a scene of flogging confusion."

She explained that Jon had called from a pay phone asking for help. He and Clancy were supposed to be finished with their adventure but the wind had blown them off schedule. They were out of food and couldn't afford the time to hitchhike into a town and resupply. Maryé agreed to meet them the next day at John Day.

In return for their help, the women were invited to ride through the locks. Laurie loved it. As the water began to pull them down and down, she thought she smelled the briny tang of the sea. The walls rose until it felt to her that the dory floated at the bottom of a giant root cellar.

She also loved what she saw in Clancy's face as the lock doors lurched open. His eyes danced between the water and the suddenly returning daylight as though gathering up all the parts of that moment. She glanced at Jon. His face wore a kindred expression. She was willing to bet they shared a common thought too, something like "Wow, isn't it great being right here, right now? Now let's ditch these women and get this show back on the road!"

She was not offended at her musings. She had often admired the connection between these two. Today it seemed to her that she, by witnessing it, shared in it.

Above the dam the day had seemed calm. But as they left its shelter, Laurie felt the first push of this wind the men had been talking about. The dory floated in calm water but just beyond the jetty that shielded the lock doors she could see waves. As Clancy rowed them out, the dory began to rock, at first gently. Then they rounded the jetty and the wind grabbed the mainsail. For an instant she thought they might tip over. The dory recovered but now it was among the waves, which were bigger than they'd looked and made the boat feel small. She braced herself with both hands. Laurie is no boatman; she tried to take her cue from Clancy and Jon. They had risen and were working to control the mainsail, but they seemed calm. She decided she would be, too.

Then Jon glanced at her and a different look flashed across his face. He began stripping off his lifejacket. She tried to protest, but the young man stared at her as though she were a child and said, "Put it on. Now." Heart racing and fingers fumbling, she did. Clancy had already passed Maryé the boat's spare. Moments later, the sail now under control, the dory began making for shore. By the time she reached the car thirty minutes later Laurie was convinced that she'd projected her own fear onto the men's faces. Those two? No way they'd spook at a few waves.

In a café that evening the men told stories about dams and barges and long wind-battered days. They looked as tired as Laurie had ever seen them.

"Sleep is for the weak, sleep is for the weak," Clancy said in a sour imitation of Jon. "I'm getting real tired of hearing that."

Laurie caught the twinkle in his eye and laughed. She also caught that he wasn't entirely kidding. Not surprising, she thought. Jon's endless energy would wear anyone down. She glanced at the younger man's unashamed grin and laughed again.

6/24/88

The fact that I'm writing this now is because we were incredibly 1. Lucky, and 2. Stupid.

After spending the day trying to drag the boat & us downstream with the water drag, with oars & with the sail, and seeing the wind waves get horribler & horribler, we did the most nearly sensible thing available. We got over to the lee side of one of the gravel islands on the side of the river & tied up to some little bush, where we stayed the day.

It was dull, but at least we got to windburn our sunburns. Jon curled up & went to sleep. I was wide awake, bored & thirsty. Half of a six pack later, I was ready for a nap.

Jon woke me at 8:00 pm. "The wind has died down."

Sure enough, it had. Conditions had gone from

unthinkable to unpleasant. There was still a stiff enough breeze to blow the top off the occasional roller, but things were apparently easing up.

We decided to try to get down the river.

We were fairly flying along on just the main and getting the miles we were after, so it didn't seem like such a bad idea. The sun was going down. The wind was rising.

About the time I decided we were trying too hard, it was later than it should have been, and the wind was going from too strong to homicidal.

It would have been stupid to be out there in daylight. We had half a moon. The waves had gone from two feet to four, with occasional sets of six plus ...

We survived because the boat is a better sailor than I am.

I was trying to steer an S course through each wave, falling off the wind on the backside of the wave & through the trough, to keep steering speed, and then back up into the wind to meet the falling face of the wave head on.

It was inevitable that I should misjudge one in the darkness, and have to take the hit quartering on the bow.

I saw it coming. I saw we weren't going to get square to it in time. I thought it would have to take us over.

In the moonlight, I could see Jon leaning over the weather rail, into the force of the wave, to help the boat keep her balance as the curl of the wave rolled over & down on us. His upper body was engulfed in spray & foam as the boat punched into & through the top & held on.

Good boat.

Jon is a good man to have with you in a tight situation. The wind & waves just kept coming—always big &

nasty with an occasional set that came hissing monstrous out of the darkness.

I may always remember that sinking feeling of falling, accelerating into those black troughs with the tops of the waves foaming overhead to crash down on us. Better to remember than to relive.

And it just kept coming and growing. I began to be afraid that even if I hit straight into the stuff it would get big enough to turn me over backwards. I would have loved to turn & run from it, but getting sideways would mean getting upside down. I didn't even suspect we'd survive if that happened.

By now the wind was fairly shrieking. I was shaking & giggling in fear and the strange exhilaration you feel as soon as you feel sure that once again it didn't quite land on you.

I guess I have been more frightened than that, though I don't like to think about it, and we aren't going to talk about it.

When we finally did get to a place on the north shore where a pumping station gave us a place to tie up to a cable, I just hung on tight to that cable for a few minutes, pretty happy to have not been killed ...We were glad to spend the rest of the night rocking around on the mooring line.

I ask Jon if he remembers being afraid that night. He thinks a bare instant. "Nope."

I ask if he's surprised at Clancy's description. He thinks longer this time. "I can see him saying that," he says slowly.

"See him being afraid?"

"He worried about water, about bad situations on water."

I instantly find myself liking the big man more.

"You don't?" I ask.

Jon laughs. "Oh, I could see it being that bad that night and me being really worried, but also pumped up, hanging over the side of the boat, reacting to each wave for whatever, 15 minutes or an hour and 15 minutes. And the next day, remembering, 'OK, we reacted, we handled it.' And forgetting that, for that hour, I was really gripped."

Worried. Gripped. But not afraid. I've yet to hear Jon use that word so I ask him about it. He tells me 'fear' describes the way he feels in a moment whose outcome is unknown. To feel fear means Jon has screwed up, has failed to manage a situation.

At Squaw Valley, the ski area where Jon patrolled as a young man, he picked up a nickname that has stuck for decades: Johnny Danger. Uncomfortable that the nickname might make him sound reckless, Jon sometimes tries to explain to people what he thinks it was meant to say about him. He started skiing at the age of five and grew up into an extreme skier with a reflexive feel for the ways snow and skis interact. Before he launches off a cornice or cliff, his mind has already landed the jump and skied it out. Part of him is already down with the bystanders, looking up at the tracks he is about to carve, knowing that they will look as he imagines them. He knows he will execute because in a sense he already has. What's so brave about that? he asks earnestly.

"I've never accomplished anything really difficult by just rolling the dice," says Jon. "People do accomplish stuff that way, but I'm a pansy. I have to know what's going to happen.

"I've accumulated enough experience that I can do stuff that seems difficult or insane, and I swear to you it could not have been easier or more enjoyable. I may take weeks or months looking at the problem. I've been shocked when people thought something I did was impressive when there's no way it couldn't have gone like I saw it."

I believe he means every word of this, but it isn't always true. It wasn't true that wild night on the Columbia. Jon knew too little of sailing and wind waves to evaluate the risks of that night. So if the young man hanging over the gunwale of the dory truly was unafraid, it was because of something he must have trusted as implicitly as himself: Clancy's big hand on the tiller.

Eleven

River's End

L ate on that wind-buffeted night in 1988, Jon Barker was startled out of his exhausted sleep. Moments later he realized he hadn't been awakened by something but by its absence.

The wind had stopped.

It was 4 a.m. when Jon slipped from his bag, cast the dory off, and began to row. It felt like magic, the pull of oar answered by the hiss of hull through calm water. Delighted, he rowed harder and harder. When Clancy finally lifted his head to look at his young friend, it was full daylight. Jon laughed down at him, "Your turn. I rowed 15 miles already."

The men rowed all through that long, calm, breathless day and far into the night, ignoring fatigue and hunger in favor of gulping down miles, afraid they might jinx themselves if they stopped.

If either had secretly begun to doubt they'd finish, the doubts ended as they rowed out the bottom of the Columbia Gorge, through the locks of the last dam, and on. When they quit that night, current again rolled beneath the dory. They were only a day from humid Portland, and beyond that, the sea.

Clancy wrote:

6/25/88

We rowed 65 miles of pond water. That pretty much covers it for the day. I mean, what else are you going to get done on a day that you row 65 fucking miles?

We got through Bonneville Lock, & over & tied up & the bags out to sleep at 2:45 a.m.

I saw Jon setting the alarm. He was setting it for 3:30! (After all, sleep is for the weak.)

We didn't get up until after 8. Rowed and sailed on down into Portland … Pulled into Salty's on Marine Drive. Real fancy yachter place. Jon & I didn't really fit in there …

Jon reads this entry aloud and laughs ruefully at the part about his alarm. "I do things like that," he says.

I've heard another version of the alarm clock story. In it, Clancy took the alarm from Jon's hand, saw that it was set to go off before dawn, and hucked the thing into the river. Jon laughs when I tell him this. He says no, Clancy didn't need to toss the clock: He had had plenty of practice at simply ignoring Jon's enthusiasms.

I've heard about the stop at Salty's elsewhere too, from Jim Hunt, an old friend of Clancy and the Barker family. Jon had called Jim to see if he wanted to meet them for a little celebration. When Jim showed up at Salty's that evening, he saw the dory tied up to the dock and went inside.

He noticed a knot of people at the bar, but didn't at first realize its cause. Then he recognized a rank but familiar smell, startling in this well-heeled yachters' club: unwashed human.

He remembers being impressed at the sight of his friends, in river shorts and stiff, filthy T-shirts, sipping rounds of free drinks in return for their story. They introduced Jim to their audience and he was welcomed as though all were long-lost friends. Jim had long appreciated that Clancy had the kind of confidence that erases social boundaries, but this tableau seemed over the top even for Clancy. Perhaps it was that the story they told was right up these yachters' alley: hellish winds and big waves; a long voyage in a handmade boat; the Pacific now within reach.

Later that night in his living room, Jim listened to Jon's descriptions of the Columbia while Clancy showered. In fresh clothes, his hair wet, Clancy walked back into the room and sat quietly a while, listening. Finally, in a tone you might employ with an obnoxious child, he interrupted Jon.

"Go take a shower," he said. "You stink."

6/27/88

Rowed/sailed on down toward Astoria—ran aground a mile from any shore after stopping to make coffee, fire, sandwiches & to let a squall pass. Rained hard for a little bit. I smelled the ocean for the first time today. There's something especially real about smell. You can see something or hear it and still be at some remove from it. When you smell it, it's there and it's real.

Saw what looked like a nice sheltered spot to camp for the night after a south tack that took over 1 1/2 hours. It was going to be dark soon & the tide was coming in, slowing our progress. Wave action was seriously against us. I was tired &

cranky. Ditto Jon.

Got safely moored. Changed clothes so we'd stink less. Took off for town & hot food. Wrong.

We had in error tied our boat to a pier at a penal colony for teenage felons-in-training. Weird shit!

This woman came up to see what was going on with us & to tell the girls to get out of the bushes. What are you doing in there, anyway?

She was one of those people that are easy to see as unlikeable if they keep quiet. She seemed to know this, and compensated by saying way too much. She was fat, ugly, stupid, loud, dressed like a colorblind schoolmarm in a thrift shop, and obviously reveled in her authority over her young, delinquent charges.

She didn't know that there was anything wrong with us leaving our boat there, but she was willing to call her superior over to see if he knew of any reason why we shouldn't be there.

Her superior was fat, ugly, stupid & dressed like a cop. He also had a prowl car—a four door AMC economy sedan with a siren.

He was very sorry he didn't know of any reason we shouldn't be there but he'd be willing to call his superior.

His superior was fat, ugly, stupid and drove a newer prowl car of the same type. He was ready to make a decision or a bluff, and was sure his superior wouldn't want us to be this close to the "residents."

By this time Jon & I were ready to leave the place and agreed we should go.

"Besides, this is all government water & a federal facility."

Jon & I agreed we should go.

"And besides, your boat isn't big enough and the Coast Guard won't let you go out over the bar in a boat that is only that big," said the fat ugly stupid thriftshop queen.

Jon & I agreed we should go.

As we got into the boat & rowed away, the F.U.S.W. was telling us she didn't want to rain on our parade, but the Coast Guard wouldn't let us do what we had rowed and sailed over 900 miles to do. Yes, indeed, it was time to leave.

By now, the tide was running back in and the wind was still against us. We didn't manage to get on into Astoria. We let the wind push us back around the peninsula of Tongue Point and on past the Tongue Point Job Corps Penal Colony. Tethered the boat to a piling & slept on the deck. At 2 a.m. heavy rain woke us—rolled up in tarps.

Daybreak—got up soggy—rowed down to Astoria. Had a tasty if small breakfast at Red Lion Inn…We walked around Astoria waiting for the tide to change—went into Knappton Barge Lines & one of the harbor pilots there called out to the pilot boat on the bar to get a firsthand report of what the ocean is doing right now out there.

"Very smooth—4 foot seas."

Right.

At the latter half of the ebb tide, we set off for what would be the end of the journey.

"That was really great. We lucked out," Jon says. "We walked in and the pilot called his boat out in the ocean and got a report on the tide, speed of the current, wind, waves, everything. And then he ran through his tide charts and said, 'You should row out at 1 p.m. today or tomorrow.' It was super."

Jon thinks a minute and adds, "The Bar was really concerning. People die out there."

The men had known from the first step of their journey that they would be ill-prepared for this, its final one. The Northwest's largest river had regained current and was in the process of narrowing from ten miles to five. In a few miles it would narrow again to two. The effect is similar to nozzling a hose.

Through that nozzle slams an average of 150 billion gallons of water each day, enough to affect ocean salinity levels as far south as San Francisco. The resulting mess is something writers call, with only a touch of hyperbole, the 'Graveyard of the Pacific.' Mapmakers call it the Columbia River Bar and mariners, simply and with respect, the Bar.

Even under calm conditions on the Bar, shoals build and shift daily, creating giant boils which seem to grow from nothing only to subside again. Whirlpools form and at their edges waves rise to pour themselves into the gaping holes. The sound is exactly like a monstrous drain.

Mostly the river rams its way into the sea, but despite jetties and regular dredging, the Pacific, with its powerful tides and fierce onshore winds, sometimes wins. Then the river is forced back onto itself and the Bar earns its nickname in spades. Outgoing river current meets incoming ocean and the long ocean swells rise into watery walls. These waves commonly exceed 20 feet. Bar pilots swear they can go 100.

Over the years, some 2,000 ships have foundered there. More than 300 were major ocean-going craft lost to storms or mechanical problems. But even on a calm day, a small boat can find itself swamped by a watery obstacle its captain never saw because only moments before it didn't exist.

The all-important channel buoys that direct deep-draft ships have been known to disappear, swallowed by the weird, conflicted forces of the place. It happens often enough that a Coast Guard team exists just to replace them. The Coast Guard located a surf rescue school here because conditions are so often ideal for training—in other words, dangerous. The nearby rescue station launches an average of 400 missions each year. In a typical year, six people die in the 48 degree waters, usually after capsizing or washing overboard from small boats.

The men knew much of this and had intended to be wary and stay near shore. But when, without incident, they passed the official mouth of the Columbia, a spot called Tongue Point, the place didn't look right for an ending to such a long and much-dreamed-of journey. Shore, though distant, still framed the water on three sides. The men had imagined that at river's end they'd be surrounded by water and sky. And anyway, Jon's map put river mile zero out on the face of the continent, not at Tongue Point. They had to cross the Bar.

Their plan was to allow the ebb tide to draw them the last 12 miles from Astoria. Then they'd wait for the flood tide to help them return against the outgoing river. What they learned from the barge pilot was this: Their plan was fine but if they wanted to cross the Bar safely their timing had to be just right. Contrary to what river intuition told them, the Bar is most dangerous not at the flood tide, the equivalent of high water on a river, but at the ebb, when the river channel is most shallow. That's when wind, river, and ocean are in greatest conflict. The pilot explained that they should use the outgoing tide as they'd planned. But it was important that they hit the dangerous waters of the Bar proper during the slack period between ebb and flood, the closest thing to calm that place sees.

As shoreline fell away on either side, the waves began to behave strangely. And to grow. These new waves built and approached from all directions, including directly beneath the boat. Almost worse, they approached at different speeds, making the dory roll in a queasy, unfamiliar rhythm. Clancy pivoted this way and that, trying to take the biggest waves bow-on, while Jon bailed. Then they switched.

The men watched the low-relief landmass of Oregon fall away until all they could see to the south was water. But to the north, the Washington side still seemed to reach beyond them into the ocean. So despite their growing nervousness they kept rowing. Nearly a thousand miles of river would mean nothing if they didn't row the last, strangest miles.

Mile zero had been easy to see on Jon's map, but out here it was not. Now they were parallel with the end of the North Jetty, a half-mile-long, eight-foot-high wall of rip-rapped boulders. Beyond the jetty they could see up the Washington coast. Was that far enough? The waves continued to grow.

That was when Clancy, bailing, scooped up the jellyfish. He tipped the bailer to show it to Jon. Neither said a word. Jellyfish don't live in rivers. The thing was done, or would be when they'd regained the safety of Ilwaco, just inside the river's mouth on the Washington side.

The men had envisioned a celebration, high fives and hollering and a toast from the pint they had brought for the purpose. But the strange waves were growing not just larger but also now more frequent and less predictable. Their moment of triumph was a word-less grin over a jellyfish and an unceremonious about-face.

On the way in, a Coast Guard patrol motored up. A guards-man hollered across the swells that he hadn't seen a boat that small cross the Bar in years. The guardsman looked them over carefully as he spoke, as though searching for a reason not to think them fools. Clancy and Jon explained quickly about the Salmon, Snake, and Columbia.

The guardsman did not seem reassured. Nor did he appear impressed and entertained, as had been the patrons of Salty's. But after promising he would keep an eye out, he and his crew motored away to let these two finish their journey.

Twelve

Anything Worth Doing

The thing was done. For Clancy Reece, I think, the story felt complete. But not for Jon Barker. The lesson of the Source to Sea exploded like a bomb in his brain: Anything you wanted to know could be known, and not out of a book or even from a map but with muscles and skin.

I imagine Clancy laughed at the fury of his young friend's passions. The older man was probably not surprised when, that winter, Jon grew obsessed with a river called the Green. Jon *was* surprised when he approached his friend about tracing that system as they had the Salmon. Clancy turned him down flat.

After all, as a human-powered voyage the Green/Colorado offered that same quixotic mix of beauty and degradation, exhilaration and drudgery as had the Salmon/Columbia. Like the Salmon, the Green begins in high, wild mountains, in this case the glacier-capped Wind Rivers of Wyoming. It runs free for 146 miles before meeting its first dam, Fontanelle. In Utah, it joins the much-exploited Colorado, which has carved a dramatic path that continues through Arizona and then California on its way to the Gulf of California. Like the Columbia, the Colorado is clogged by massive reservoirs. But not completely. Early Colorado River activists had fought for and won a few freeflowing segments, including the Grand Canyon, perhaps the most famous wilderness whitewater trip in the world.

Jon had done his homework, paying particular attention to accounts of Major John Wesley Powell's famous 1869 exploration of the river system. It appeared that, as with the Salmon, nobody, not even Powell, had put the whole thing together from headwaters to ocean.

Nights in the ski patrol dorm room that winter he lay awake. Nobody had traced the Green entire. It begged to be done. Jon could not understand why Clancy did not also feel compelled to go, but after more sleepless nights Jon decided he would do it anyway.

In September of 1989 he launched. He used a combination of inflatable kayak, hardshell kayak, and raft. His girlfriend, Cate Casson, provided road support. She and another raft guide joined him for some segments but more often Jon boated alone. The journey stretched across more than 70 days and 1,700 river miles. Paddling across those massive reservoirs was as tediously difficult a thing as Jon had ever done. One, the famous Lake Powell, is 168 miles long. It took three days to cross it.

The Colorado's dams have no locks to pass through so Jon decided he would nudge his kayak up against their tops before he paddled to shore and carried his kayak around. At Hoover Dam this got him detained, but after the earnest young boater explained his mission, the officer not only released him but helped him carry his boat through a locked gate that guarded the river below.

Near its terminus, the Colorado unravels into a confusing sprawl of manmade canals, some dewatered, some navigable. At one point Jon and Cate drove back and forth along 40 miles of what had once been river before they found a canal he could relaunch onto.

Along the way, although he didn't know it until the man's book came out, Jon passed his competition. Another adventurer was tracing the river system top to bottom, also imagining himself first. The contemplative Colin Fletcher's voyage took six months rather than 70 days, despite the motor he used to cross those interminable reservoirs.

On a shrunken planet where nearly every mountain bears bootprints and every mile of river has been run, being 'first' tends to require creative task definition. Fletcher's book about his journey, called *River*, allowed that both men had been first. Fletcher argued he was first because he backpacked the 40 miles Jon drove, and because he had no road support. Jon, Fletcher said, was also first. Jon finished first. Also, unlike Fletcher's, Jon's water miles were all human-powered.

For me such small distinctions call into question that whole, long tradition of resting the value of an adventurer's story on its 'firstness,' but I expect Jon to care. When I ask him about Fletcher and his book though, he shrugs impatiently. What Jon wants to talk about are rivers.

After the Green/Colorado Jon spent a season in Africa guiding on the world-famous Zambezi River for an adventure rafting company called Sobek. This was barely a decade after that monster river's first descent by Sobek founder Richard Bangs and colleagues. On Bangs' exploratory trip, five boats had flipped and one man's raft had been attacked and partially deflated by a crocodile, all in 60 short miles of river.

About this time Jon set the 20 new rivers goal he was still pursuing when I met him in his farmhouse more than a decade later. After Africa it led him to South America, where he could easily meet quota by bouncing from jungle river to jungle river.

Jon's South American adventures included a first descent of a little-known Peruvian river called the Cotahuasi. More than most rivers, the Cotahuasi had major motion picture-style ingredients: difficult access; encounters with remote tribes to whom the neoprene-clad rafters apparently seemed as strange as if they'd spiraled into their villages on giant wings; and an unscoutable, forbidding canyon section which locals swore was unrunnable. Luckily the locals were wrong. The canyon was runnable, if just barely.

In 1995 Jon and his friends returned for a first descent of the Cotahuasi's largest tributary, the Rio Maran. The adventurers, recognizing the romantic marketability of these rivers, tried to find sponsors for their Peruvian explorations and even produced a VHS documentary, but self-promotion was a tougher game than they'd imagined and they quickly decided that attempts to fund expeditions got in the way of enjoying them.

Clancy didn't join Jon for any of these adventures either. His river love affair with the Salmon was, it seemed, monogamous.

But there were adventures on Clancy's beloved Salmon to compel Jon, even over the roar of the Zambezi. Each spring that the Salmon ran high, for instance, Jon and usually Clancy planned an assault on the Slide, the rapid that had stopped them for one long week on their Source to Sea voyage. At high flows that rapid is considered unrunnable, but these two weren't looking for high flows. They wanted massive, even insane flows. Not 20,000 cubic feet per second, the safety cutoff for most rafters, but 40,000 and 60,000 and higher if possible.

At such extreme levels the rapid is a behemoth, the kind

of water rafters look at and, although they can't help imagining themselves running it, also can't stop imagining with utter clarity the pummeling they'd receive if they tried.

No ordinary raft could navigate such a rapid. It would be swallowed—before it even encountered the rapid proper—by the massive entry wave. So the men borrowed one of Jon's dad's huge army surplus pontoon rafts, long as a two-story building and powered by an outboard motor. Each person wore two lifejackets although they were not sure even double flotation would save them if they swam. The water was too aerated, too chaotic. Even the eddies, the calmest water in most rapids, surged as if huge sea monsters battled beneath.

Jon usually enlisted someone to film these Slide runs or did it himself, eventually accumulating a library of the many-faced rapid's incarnations. In the videos, the size of those waves is impossible to judge until the huge pontoon raft appears and is folded, twisted, and pushed into near-vertical tailstands, but all the runs are clean. No flips, no swims. The only swimmer in the Slide collection is Jon, the year he decided to duplicate the giant pontoon boat's successful run in a tiny inflatable kayak.

Jon's most grueling river project was something his friends ended up calling the 5X5. This one also involved the Salmon, so Clancy involved himself. The idea was to demonstrate how uniquely whitewater-blessed Idaho is by running 100 miles each on five wild-water rivers during spring flood *in five consecutive days*.

Where else but Idaho, Jon explains earnestly, could you find five whitewater rivers long enough for a 100-mile run; forceful enough to push a boat through those segments in a single day each; completely navigable through that 100-mile span so that no time was wasted on portages; within driving distance of each other; and all but one undammed so that spring melt pumped them full and fast? It was practically begging to be done, he says with absolutely no irony.

Clancy came along for three stretches: the Middle Fork of the Salmon, the Main Salmon and the Snake. Jon's dad and several other friends made up the rest of the crew, but only Jon completed the entire marathon, driving through the nights, launching before dawn each day and rowing nearly until dusk. *Paddler Magazine*, the whitewater community's biggest periodical and an advocate of envelope-pushing, carried an article on the stunt. Its tone was admiring but amused. Even in the world of hardcore boaters, Jon apparently paddled a bit far from the main current.

And so the years passed. Clancy and Jon tried but could not think up the sequel to their idyllic 1988 journey. The Source to Sea had brewed in Clancy's mind for much of his life. Jon had wanted it from his teens. Tracing the length of the Salmon and then rowing out onto the Pacific had been a pinnacle achievement, a perfect blending of everything they valued, separately and together. What would even come close?

For Clancy, a fitting sequel would have to feel significant. "Anything worth doing is worth overdoing" was a fine motto, but it wasn't the overdoing part that mattered most to him. For Jon, it would have to be a first. For both, it had to celebrate the Salmon—its power, wildness, great length, the fact that the river was undammed, and most of all, the fact that they each knew it like an old friend.

Marathon-style boating—overdoing, in other words—was interesting to both men as long as the narrative behind it was compelling. For people who have spent much of their lives moving at the speeds muscle and gravity can generate, a 100-mile day seems like a wonderful collapsing of time and space. But even Jon had to admit that his 5X5 had not had the magic of that month-long voyage to the Pacific. He began to wonder if anything would again.

On their annual fall raft trips on the Snake, which for Jon were about hiking all the major ridges reaching up from the river and, for Clancy, about fishing as he floated through a canyon gone quiet in the October chill, they batted ideas back and forth. One year Clancy tossed a new question at Jon. If you liked the idea of rowing as far as you could in a day, didn't the distance that could be traveled depend on what you decided was the length of a day? Did a day, for instance, *have* to end at dusk?

Clancy captured his own imagination with that question. He loved to launch on moonlit summer nights. If he was alone he fished. If he was with friends he talked, listened to the night, drank a few beers, and fished. He told one friend that what he loved about nighttime floats was the transformation of the known into the mysterious. At night, knife-edged shadows cleave cliff walls that stretch unbroken in sunlight. At night, whitecaps glow from within, marking the otherwise invisible waves. Overfamiliar rapids regain their ability to surprise. River segments so popular that they can't be floated in solitude become, as they were when Clancy first fell in love with them, private places.

Jon became consumed. As soon as he got home the maps came out, mileages were calculated, river gradient studied. June had the fewest hours of full darkness, maybe six. So what six-hour section was safe enough to reserve for night, when any rapids it held would have to be run by spotlight? When should they put in, at dawn? Midday? Dusk?

Of course, said Jon, talking fast, it wouldn't be worth doing if they didn't row as hard as they possibly could. But no matter how hard they rowed, most of the speed would come from the current. Hard rowing only bought a mile or two per hour over current speed. Which meant you needed maximum current. If you were going to set a record you should set it as high as you could.

So what they should do, said Jon, was launch on the bubble, the highest flow of the year, on the West's last big, free river, and ride the magical moment in which the Salmon does what few major rivers in the world are allowed to do anymore: run amok.

Clancy listened to his friend's gears spin up, smiled his quiet smile. He didn't care about how or when. He was 50 years old. It was long past time to do something big again. All he had to say was yes, and he could spend the winter contemplating this upcoming journey against the backdrop of a life of journeys. He could restore his dory, which had fallen into a disrepair that pained him, just as he had once spent a winter dreaming a big adventure and building it.

Yes, said Clancy. Let's do it. My dory. Your plan. At the roaring peak of high water when the Salmon is transformed into a muscular, experts-only river, let's see how far we can row in a single, 24-hour day, never stopping, never resting, through darkness and out the other side.

Part II

Thirteen

Viking Funeral

June 15, 1996

A microphone hangs by its cord at the river's edge. The day is warm; beer and pop overflow from coolers into hands. A row of wood and fiberglass dories are hauled up side by side on shore, chummy as basking sea lions, rendering even more solitary the boat that surges alone, at anchor, out in the eddy. This solitary boat is different from those ashore in several ways. The most obvious is that it has a mast.

Flecks of color, all the flowers that could be harvested from the yards of tiny Riggins, Idaho, spin on the brown water. Beyond, the swollen river's main current charges along.

From the river's edge rises a massive ponderosa pine, its roots in water, its crown dark against the crystalline sky. A man could not reach around its trunk to touch his own fingers. It's beneath this tree that the microphone waits and the people come, one by one.

Most face the crowd to talk. Some stare at the boat in the eddy, as if addressing an invisible someone seated in the rowing compartment.

"We all wanted to be as much like him in abilities and attitudes toward life and the river as possible," a man reads from a piece of paper he holds between himself and the crowd. It sounds like he's forcing his words through a plug of damp sand. The man's name is Mike Kennedy. Once, before he met a man named Clancy Reece, he had been a farmer in Nebraska.

This man recites a long poem he has titled, "The Boatman River King." Parts are supposed to be funny. The crowd laughs encouragingly.

Another man comes to the microphone with a guitar slung over his shoulder. Several minutes later he has not yet sung his song, is still talking, apparently helpless to stop. "Clancy never imitated himself, that man never imitated himself once. He was as he was," sobs the man.

It's an odd-looking crowd for a funeral. Some of the 200-plus attendees wear jeans but most are in baggy nylon shorts, ballcaps, and T-shirts. Some, like the poem reader, wear cowboy hats. Sport sandals are the nearly universal footwear.

One man's dress stands out even here. Under a leather loin-cloth, he wears sweat pants scissored off at mid-calf for wading. On his bare chest hangs a small leather medicine bag. High on one biceps is an armband of inch-long, ivory-white objects. Perhaps they are claws. His cowboy hat sprouts an eagle feather. Nobody gives him a second glance, as though he dresses this way every day, which he does.

This man's name is Gary Lane. He says, "Smoke jumpers have a saying. All men die, but a few learn to live before they die. Clarence was such a man."

Clarence. Clancy. A few call the dead man Twerp. A stranger listening to the amplified voices—for instance any of the half-dozen law enforcement types clumped uncomfortably on the dirt road—would glean from the stories these names, as well as a few details: Clancy had been a strong man, and both he and his friends had been proud of his strength. He had taught many of those present about fishing, rapids and rivers. He had enjoyed people but also, more than most, enjoyed being alone.

What could be read between the lines, perhaps better by an outsider than by those grieving here, is that much of these people's pain derives from the fact that this man, this Clancy Reece, has been a touchstone for them, and that both the fact and manner of his death are at odds with what he has come to represent.

They tell how Clancy wrote, shared books, smoked pot, and philosophized on river banks. They remember how he would walk out of sight and then the birdlike voice of his recorder, an instrument like a flute, would come curling through camp on the breeze. They talk about how he floated Idaho rivers at flood and drought, under moonlight and summer sun, for money and for fun, alone and with friends, year after year after year, always with relish, always aware. He was so strong that several present had seen him snap oars simply by hauling on them too hard. So clear-eyed that when he looked at a problem he simultaneously saw a web of solutions. So restrained that although he had little patience for those who didn't see as well as he did, only his closest friends were privy to the fact. So tough that, goaded into fights by some injustice or another, he reminded one man of "a lawnmower in a pile of rocks."

The man in the loincloth tells about a night under a full moon at a place called Saddle Creek on the Snake. He had watched from shore as Clancy rowed out alone into the big standing waves alongside the camp eddy. "All you could see," the man says, "was a black silhouette, this Charles Atlas out in this dory boat, surfing this wave."

The audience nods in rapt agreement as though each had been there, standing on slick river rock, surrounded by darkness, each the sole and silent witness to a man's dance with a river.

The six or so uniformed men that stand awkwardly apart from this crowd are Forest Service, Bureau of Land Management, sheriff's deputies, or maybe all three, since at least that many agencies' regulations are about to be broken, and the officers' original purpose in coming here was to prevent that from happening.

When they arrived, or so the story goes, they had been met by a large bald man.

"Seems to me there's more of us than there are of you," the bald man had announced, his tone all friendly good advice. "So either go get more of you, or stay here and be quiet and polite."

Which, the officers had probably realized, was a fair assessment. Or maybe it has gotten to them, this casual yet hyperbolic ritual. Either way, they make no move when, just after sundown, the thing they came here to prevent begins.

Three men get into a dory and pull away from shore. The oarsman is the wearer of the loincloth. In the bow perches a short, dark man. The dory circles with the current until it intercepts the boat with the mast, the boat anchored alone in the river. The short man steps over and busies himself aboard.

The dory upon which he is occupied has strange lines, a little too long and slim for a whitewater craft. Despite its mast, however, it is also a little too wide and squat for a sailboat.

While the man on the dory works, people continue to come to the mike, but they are distracted and edgy. One man positions himself, arms crossed, in front of the dories tied ashore. His name is Bruce Elmquist. Once he was a guide trainee under Clancy Reece.

Before that, he was a hippie who accepted a raft ride through Hells Canyon's biggest rapid and stepped from that raft changed. He stares belligerently at the clump of law enforcement. The officers make no move, so after a few minutes he relaxes, picks up his beer, turns to watch with everyone else the man working out in the river.

Finally, the man waves his ride back in. Over the mike a voice announces what most already know, "This would be a really good time to cover your ears …"

A minute later, hot orange light flashes from the vicinity of the mast, followed by a concussion that shivers the air. Silence returns. Amazingly, the boat appears unaffected, although smoke now wreaths the mast like a ghost sail.

Seconds later another flash and blast of sound originate from somewhere beneath the gunwales. This time the boat bucks like a shot deer. The mast shudders, sags tiredly into the water, swirls out of sight. The dory still bobs at anchor, tugging on its rope, but now it has a disturbing, wounded look.

On shore people are hurrying into lifejackets, jumping into the waiting dories. These people are not historians and they don't know much about Viking funerals, but they know two things: First, Clancy Reece had often said that when he died he wanted such a funeral; and second, in a Viking funeral the boat—and the fallen warrior—do not smoke.

They burn.

Which is why diesel-soaked driftwood fills the dory to its gunwales, and why the dories rowing out from shore, nearly invisible in the half-darkness, carry unlit torches. As the first torch is lit, fire sparkles on the waves and makes molten a thin band of water that reaches for shore. The torch is tossed aboard the crippled dory and immediately a thicker band of light paints itself onto the water. A second and third torch land upon the pyre. The last dory lights its torch from the burning bow and carries flame to the stern.

Moments later the slim dory is transformed into a startling, magical thing, a boatful of fire. This is not gentle magic: Flames claw upward into the air, fanned high by a stiff upstream wind. At first people howl and whistle in appreciation, but the noise dies fast. Destruction is a hard thing to celebrate.

For a long time the boat burns. Evening becomes night and nobody comes forward to pick up the mike and resume telling stories. Finally darkness is complete except for the flames on the river. When the dories circling the fiery boat pass behind it, their riders' solemn faces become visible. They cross before it as stark silhouettes and then, when the current swings their orbits wide, they disappear altogether, only to appear again behind the flames. What they don't do, for a very long time, is leave the burning dory alone.

Finally the white noise of the river is broken by a man's voice, amplified by the microphone. He sings a slow, sad hymn. His amateurish reach for the high notes imparts a vulnerable grace to what could have been a maudlin gesture.

The dory's hull begins to lose integrity. Fiery cracks reach down its sides; flames drip into the water. More time passes and now the quieting fire seems to sit on the water itself. Low voices express pleasure at the boat's durability. It *should* take a long time to destroy a man's proudest possession.

Then a new voice begins to talk over the sound system. It belongs to a man named Jon Barker. It quickly becomes clear that this man feels responsible for the events of this night and that he wants to help people feel better. He tells stories from his childhood, when Clancy was a young man. He does not tell the story nobody else could, the story whose ending has brought them all here.

Earlier in the afternoon, wood had been gathered for a riverbank bonfire, but apparently the crowd agrees there should be only one fire in the night. Nobody moves to light the stacked wood. Jon and the storytellers who follow him are voices from the dark.

Finally the dory fire sinks to embers and then to nothing. Protected by water, however, the hull bottom has survived. Under cover of darkness it frees itself and escapes the eddy. Two hundred people tell stories beside the river while the hull drifts downstream, invisible as a ghost, black on black.

Black on black it tumbles through a rapid called Ruby, thought unrunnable at high water until, many years ago, or so the story goes, Clancy pioneered the route. Eventually it drifts into Riggins, a town now calling itself Idaho's Whitewater Capital and chock-full of rafting companies, although once it was a dying mill town. The hull settles into a huge curve which locals call the Wood Eddy because they collect winter fuel from the driftwood that gets caught in the powerful revolving currents there. Raft guides, hunting for different booty, call it Six-Pack Eddy.

Which is where Jack Kappas, an old dory guide turned Bureau of Land Management river ranger, found it. Clancy was Jack's hero as well. Against his superiors' wishes, Jack had attended the Viking funeral. Days later when he saw the low, black shape awash in the eddy, he knew immediately what it was. He pulled the hull from the water and hauled it far above the high water line.

Where it rests today, a nondescript bit of flotsam for those who don't know its story, a fitting marker for those who do.

Fourteen

"It Should Be a Wild Ride"

May, 1996

W eeks earlier and halfway across Idaho, in the capital city of Boise, Mary Mellema picked up the phone, becoming part of the story that ends with that burned hull.

She recognized the quiet voice. If she'd had a moment to enjoy idle thoughts lately, she might have anticipated it. After all, a major runoff event was shaping up across Idaho, and this Jon Barker person was eternally, infernally interested in high water.

It was May and Mary Mellema was the Idaho hydrologist for the National Weather Service. Her job was to forecast the seasonal rise and fall of Idaho rivers, and to sound the alarm when there was not enough water, or like this year, when there was going to be too much.

Snowmelt, not rainfall, supplies most of the surface water in the dry Northern Rockies and Intermountain West. Water crises build slowly, like thunderheads on the horizon. This year, it was becoming apparent that many Idaho rivers—in particular the Salmon, whose huge granitic catchment was still buried in heavy snowcover—were going to run big. A dozen times a century big.

Until recently, Mary's clients had been Idaho water managers. She helped them decide how much water to release from reservoirs around the state so that mountain meltwater would fill but not overflow them. She also predicted the occasional spring flood event and the more typical summer drought.

Water managers downstream in Washington called mostly to ask about a single river, the Salmon. The Columbia and lower Snake are run like a factory. This factory's products are power, commercial navigation, and cheap irrigation water. Variables that might interfere with efficient operation are not welcomed, and the Salmon is such a variable. Every other river that supplies significant water to the Columbia is dammed. So one of Mary's most important jobs each year was to guess how much water the wild card Salmon would deliver.

Mary's job was less like crystal-ball gazing than it might sound. Nobody can say with certainty whether it will rain on a given spot on a certain day. But big patterns, even complicated ones, can be sketched with reasonable reliability if you have enough data. Mary had at her disposal nearly a century's worth of regional weather observations and corresponding river behavior. She had access to weather data from remote sensing stations scattered across the region, including far out in the Pacific. And thanks to the United States Department of Agriculture's snow telemetry or SNOTEL network, she knew exactly what was going on in the all-important snowpack.

SNOTEL involves very sci-fi-sounding technology. Situated high in the region's major catchments, SNOTEL sites are unmanned stations that monitor snow depth and density. Most of these sites are too remote for either satellite or cellular transmission of their data—satellite is too expensive and cellular too short-range and unreliable. The solution that made the whole system possible was a technology called meteor burst transmission.

It turns out that meteors too small to be visible to the eye cross the sky every few minutes. Each has an ion tail much like a jet's contrail. SNOTEL sites communicate with a central receiver by bouncing data off of these ion trails. Each meteor's tail can serve this purpose for no more than a second, but that doesn't matter. When a tail fades, the station simply goes silent until the next meteor passes.

The West is so thirsty that it has been considered reasonable to capture entire rivers and transport them hundreds of miles—allowing their native drainages to die—in the name of human thirst. That thirst drove the demand for accurate projections of water availability, too.

In recent years, a new kind of client had begun making use of SNOTEL and other water data: river recreationists. Lately they made up half of Mary's incoming calls. These were not the people the system had been designed to serve: The information they wanted had nothing to do with large-stroke patterns. It was specific. Often it was personal.

One caller would be concerned about his coveted Selway launch. The Selway is a wilderness river, access to which is controlled by a permit system. Permits are awarded by a long-odds lottery: That year, 1996, nearly 1,700 people applied for the 62 permits.

But landing a permit is only the first of a would-be floater's hurdles. The Selway becomes extremely hazardous at high flows, and many consider it unrunnably rocky when low. The river is also notoriously variable. It can jump overnight to flows so high that a cautious boater would cancel his once-in-a-lifetime trip. The worried caller might tell Mary he was trying to decide whether to rent a more maneuverable boat or cancel.

Or an outfitter might call as he wrestled with whether to cancel a sold-out trip on southern Idaho's Owyhee. The Owyhee is a desert river that burns through its meager, low elevation snowpack early. Some years rafts scrape across shallow rocks even during peak runoff. The outfitter's question has been keeping him up nights: At what rate will the water drop? Canceling a commercial trip at the last second can be a disaster for a small business owner. Running the trip without enough water to float a boat is worse.

The fact that these new customers were not the people the system was designed to serve was a moot point for Mary Mellema. She'd provide the best forecasts she could to whoever called. That was the job.

Forecasting for this Jon Barker person was especially time consuming. This time of year, he'd want to know when and how high a river, usually the Salmon, would peak. But not just which week or even which day. He'd ask which part of the day, and exactly what she thought the peak flow would be. Then he'd get even more specific. If the water peaked at the Whitebird gage at 3 p.m. on a given day, he might ask, when had that bubble of high water passed a particular spot 200 miles upstream?

Unlike most callers, this one also wanted to know how she arrived at her forecasts. He seemed nearly as interested in raw data and how she processed it as she was. When she wasn't busy, she enjoyed the man's questions. He seemed to understand that it was the data that was real. Forecasts were just that, her reaching out before herself, with help from accumulated patterns, to make educated guesses.

But Jon Barker seldom called when she wasn't busy. He called, like today, when the rivers were pulsing upward and every agency she served was on alert.

Talking to me at her dining table six years later, Mary expresses surprise that she remembers so much about Jon Barker's phone calls that hectic spring of 1996. She supposes part of the reason is that for several weeks that year he called every day, always asking the same three questions about the Salmon: when; how high; and how sure was she? But perhaps it was also that her conversations with him made her feel, despite herself, somehow connected to what later happened to Jon Barker and his friends on the river. Was it her job to help people put themselves in harm's way?

For Jon's part, Mary had become a prized resource the first time he called her at the recommendation of another outfitter. A careful scientist with a passion for natural systems, Mary Mellema had impressed Jon with her willingness to provide the exhaustive detail he craved.

So now, every January, he'd call to ask, "How does the Owyhee basin snowpack stack up to this time last year?" And she would *not* say, "Gee, as I recall, pretty close to the same." Instead she'd put him on hold. When she returned, she'd rattle off averages, exceedances and percentages until Jon had all the information he could want.

Which is saying something. Jon can spout the high flows on the Salmon for the last century. This is not a feat of prodigious memory. He reviews that data the way many people watch television: to relax, to set his mind ambling along a familiar path. If you name a year, he can recall some interesting bit of Salmon River data to go with it.

Mary had decided early on that the man was an amateur hydrologist and his questions were academic. Why would anyone, even the most avid floater, need that kind of detail? What would anyone actually *do* with information about when in a diurnal cycle a flooding river peaked? She figured he probably generated his own kitchen table forecasts and then called her to check his work. Sometimes, truth be told, it felt like he was keeping score on her.

Then, that first Friday in June of 1996, he told her the reason for his barrage of recent calls. His interest was not academic. He planned to raft the Salmon as close to its peak as possible and thereby set some kind of speed record. Mary wasn't sure how she felt about that.

But answering questions was her job. "If I were a betting woman, I'd say this weekend," she told him.

"That's kinda what I thought," he said. Then, as always, he pressed her further. Saturday or Sunday? What part of the day? How high? If she wasn't willing to say with any assurance now, would she be in the office on the weekend?

Exasperated, Mary explained that the office was closed weekends, and that he had already gotten the best forecast she could give. And then she relented. One more time she got out her graphs and weather data. The snowpack on Banner Summit, the most predictive SNOTEL site for the Salmon, was 'cooked,' or 'ripe,' as hydrologists like to say. This meant that it held as much meltwater as it possibly could, some 40 to 45 percent. The other key to a fast, hard runoff was weather and sure enough, clear skies and record high temperatures were predicted for the weekend. Lows in the high country would stay well above freezing. That was the kind of weather that melts a month's worth of winter in a few days, sends it sheeting down mountainsides and into the Salmon.

And for the last time, she gave him her best guess: On Sunday, the Salmon would peak at 100,000 cubic feet per second. That was nearly double the river's normal spring high and ten times its typical midsummer flow. It would peak in a massive flush, as it did perhaps a dozen times in a century.

"Ok, I think we're going to go for it," he said. "It should be a wild ride." Even six years later, she remembers that after he spoke, he laughed happily.

Monday, as always, her first stop when she arrived at the office was at the readouts. She thought of it as playing Monday morning quarterback. The Whitebird gage on the Lower Salmon registered a weekend high of 96,000 cfs. The voice on the phone had gotten what he'd been after. She hoped he'd been prepared for it.

And she gave it no more thought. Not then anyway. This was her busiest season and she had work to do.

Fifteen

Speed Run: Launch

June 8, 1996

I t was Saturday afternoon by the time Jon Barker, Clancy Reece and a last-minute addition named Craig Plummer reached the Deer Gulch launch. The long drive from Lewiston and the unseasonable warmth had made the men sleepy. Jon had allotted two hours for rest before their push-off time, so after they rigged Clancy's dory he set his alarm and the men lay in the shade of the truck to nap. They'd launch that evening and, with any luck, ride Mary Mellema's predicted bubble all the way.

New leaves rustled high in the cottonwoods, their undersides flashing silver. Riverbank sumac exuded that tangy smell that goes hand-in-hand with spring and high water on the Salmon. Current hissed through brushy willows that would, in a month, be rooted in dry ground.

Although he felt as revved up as a kid on Christmas Eve, Jon forced himself to doze.

The normally happy-go-lucky Craig could not. For kicks, he had done a few legs of Jon's 5X5 river marathon after asking around about Barker, whom he'd known of but not really known. What he'd been told was, if you were going to get involved in Jon's stunts, Jon was a good guy to get involved in them with. The 5X5 had gone fine, so here Craig was, ready—OK, mostly ready—to follow Jon into another whitewater epic.

But this one felt different. He couldn't shake the feeling that it was disrespectful to venture onto a floodstage wilderness river without extra precautions. Yet here they were, stripping precautions away. They would launch alone, at night, in a wooden boat.

Craig was a rafter, accustomed to the reassuring bulk of an air-filled craft. To his eye, Clancy's slim handmade dory looked fragile—and sinkable. He didn't like the dory's oar setup either. He ran his own boat with the oars rigidly attached to the frame and the blades held perpendicular to the water, a set-up boaters call pins and clips. Clancy's boat was rigged old-school: The oar shafts sat loosely in locks shaped like horseshoes. Open oarlocks feel precarious to those unaccustomed to them because the set-up doesn't prevent a critical oar stroke from being twisted into an ineffectual swat. Still, Craig loved rafting and good times. At the heart of this thing was a whitewater river and a boat. How bad could it get?

As evening cooled the air, the men rose and stowed their small parcels of personal gear in the hatches. They had brought only necessities: a spotlight and battery; Jon's notes and map; jugs of water and chocolate milk; ziplock bags crammed with takeout pizza; extra lifejackets; and inflatable pads for the sleep they'd more than deserve when they finished. On deck were the blue plastic-coated aluminum oars, the safety rope and the bailer. The boat was without sail, rudder or keel, stripped and graceful with its freshly painted, red-trimmed white exterior and gunship gray interior.

Jon surveyed the scene with satisfaction. Here, above all of its major tributaries, the river was small, not much wider than the quiet two-lane highway that paralleled it. But even here it was obvious that 1996 was no ordinary high water year. The concrete boat ramp was almost completely underwater. The river clicked by at a swift, brown seven miles per hour, every few minutes bearing a full-sized tree.

Upon that turbulence the dory looked like an old friend. Jon had spent some 70 days in Clarence's handmade boat, between the Source to Sea and other, less ambitious adventures. He was glad they would use it for this project, setting a world record with it that none outside their circle would care—or even hear—about. He also understood that the boat floating high and light before them was the thing that made this project make sense to Clarence.

The purity and minimalism of this trip, evidenced by that stripped-down, solo boat, satisfied Jon in the same way fast and light 'alpine style' mountaineering, which also relies on skill and speed, satisfies its advocates. He felt a pleasant buzz. This trip, which had been planned with endless attention to detail, was about to become action, exertion, and eventual success. He glanced at his old friend. He knew Clarence was amused by his compulsive attention to times, distances, maps. It had made his decision to participate in this time-driven adventure a pleasant surprise, and an affirming one.

Clancy, eyeing his dory, bright white against the high-water brown of the river, must have felt something more complicated, perhaps an ambivalent pride. He was a man of dreams. He wanted to sail this dory down Hells Canyon's biggest rapids, running the steepest, Granite, at the stroke of midnight. He had inventions to get rich by, business ventures to launch. He made restless plans to fix up the old motorcycle in his shed, make wine from the grapes ripening on his back fence, build a stereo system, write a book.

But unlike Jon, who could not separate dreaming from doing, Clancy found pleasures of the moment at least as compelling as sustained striving. Freedom and dreaming were satisfying in themselves. His friends had learned to expect him mostly when he wasn't expected. When he stayed overnight at their houses he slept outside, unwilling to give up even the small measure of autonomy that a guest relinquishes in return for hospitality. And although he believed in the sanctity of a man's word and the value of a solid day's work, he might say he'd show up at the Barker warehouse at noon and not arrive until 1 or 2 p.m.—or the next day.

These things had always been more or less true, but he no longer bore their costs as lightly as he once had, especially the lack of financial security. And there was also this: Clancy would turn 51 in a few days. He occasionally seemed startled at the failings of the middle-aged, increasingly overweight body he now inhabited.

It seemed just yesterday that, young and indestructible, silently awhirl with ideas, he'd spent a winter with the wizened hermit of the Salmon River, Sylvan 'Buckskin Bill' Hart. The little man had lived in roadless wilderness at a place called Five Mile Bar. He'd forged guns and knives, medieval-style armor and a mini-castle. He'd built bridges and two cabins and an irrigation system for his fields. Rafters gave him food and supplies in return for tours and stories. For them, the clever hermit was a novelty. Writers billed him as 'the last mountain man.' But Clancy knew what Hart really was: an expatriate hiding out inside his country.

The winter Clancy had stayed with the old man, Hart had helped him forge two knives. They became prized possessions. The men had had a lot in common: Both had earned college degrees they never capitalized on. Both valued their time far too much to trade much of it for money or even for companionship.

But the young Clancy Reece had known he didn't want to become Buckskin Bill. He was no expatriate. He liked the American dream, especially its promise of tangible reward for intelligence and motivation. Yet somehow after all these years, this boat, rough of construction but pretty of line, was the most tangible thing he owned. And it was a thing nobody but a guy like Clancy would want.

The rest of it—the uncounted thoughtful conversations and solitary moments; the million perfect casts, monofilament line arcing over the water; the thousands of lovely trout boated; the hundred exquisitely-timed runs through Wild Sheep Rapids; the handful of crackerjack guides he'd trained who were now training other generations—those were not things a man could wrap his arms around.

So in the end hadn't he become that old mountain man after all, proud but perilously close to extraneous, full of esoteric knowledge the broader world found colorful more than useful?

Perhaps all this had been on his mind through the spring as he worked on the boat, patching, sanding, and painting. Even when it began to look as though he would run out of time to finish his repairs, he insisted on using his dory for this trip, arguing speed but also rightness. This was the craft that had taken him and Jon to the sea almost ten years earlier. He seemed so fixated on his task that people at the Barker warehouse teased him: Mellow Clancy had morphed into driven Jon.

It must have felt good to bring youth back to his dory, a gift he could not give himself. If you've let physical power and prowess be the engine upon which plan A depends, what do you do when the engine slows? If you are Clancy Reece, you muscle it into obedience. But that won't work forever and you know it, just as you know you never got around to a plan B.

Put-in was scheduled for 8:50 p.m. Pacific. A little after 8 p.m. Craig donned heavy fleece and his dry suit, its rubber gaskets uncomfortably tight at ankles, wrists and neck. Jon did the same. Craig was surprised when Clancy did not. That rubber raingear the big man pulled on instead? Fine for a walk in the rain, but a joke if you swam. Maybe the man didn't own a drysuit. He seemed like the type, that old-fashioned, too-tough-for-Goretex type. But Jon had brought the guy a neoprene wetsuit. Craig watched Clancy take it from him and, without comment, stow it in a hatch.

Craig was not taking any such chances. He'd wear his drysuit every second of this run, in the chill of the coming night but also through the heat of the next day. That water was cold enough to kill. He'd also carry beneath his drysuit the necessities of life: a Swiss Army knife, lighter and extra cigarettes.

Then something struck Craig. The other reason Clancy stowing that wetsuit looked odd was that you just didn't see people tell Jon no.

It had happened on the 5X5 too, come to think of it. The evening before their first launch, they had dropped the boat over a roadside snowbank into the river, tied it fast, and begun to make camp on the least unappetizing spot they could find, a room-sized circle of wet ground completely ringed by sodden snowdrifts. As darkness fell, bringing brutal cold, there had been talk of making a fire.

Jon had argued that no, what they needed was sleep. They would rise before dawn and the day would be long. They'd be warm enough in their bags. The men grumbled but seemed to accept Jon's judgment. Clancy, who had taken no part in the discussion, walked off. He returned from the darkness with an armload of wood and, without a word, laid and lit a fire. Jon accepted the mutiny with good humored frustration. Craig figured that was their deal.

At 8:45, Clancy took the rowing seat. Craig climbed gingerly aboard, the dory dipping under his weight.

Jon came aboard last, eyeing the wristwatch he only carried when time mattered, in other words only when he wanted to time himself on a river or hike. He pushed the nose gently off the bank. Clancy caught his eye. Jon knew what was coming.

"Anything worth doing," the big man said. "Is worth overdoing."

It was the kind of joke that, unaccountably, gets funnier as it wears thin. Clancy had been saying it as long as anybody could recall. It had become the line his friends used when they wanted to mimic him. For Jon, though, it had come to mean something serious: It was the basis of their friendship. Sometimes Jon was hard put to say why these adventures, these 'projects,' mattered so much to him. But he knew that many of them also mattered to this man.

Eyes on his watch, Jon signaled. Clancy gave two solid oar-strokes, the men leaning to counter the sudden push of current as the dory crossed the eddy line, and the journey began. It was exactly 8:50 p.m.

Sixteen

Through the Night

As the hills to their left darkened, the current and Clancy's powerful oarstrokes swept them toward their lengthening shadows. Then the sun left the water and suddenly it was evening.

The plan was to row nonstop, the oarsman facing backward for the extra power in that stroke, each oarstroke from each man as strong as he could make it, for an hour or until he felt himself slowing. Then a fast switch, no strokes missed if possible, and a chance to splash sweat from the face, grab a slug of water, fold a piece of cold pizza into the mouth, body first cooling and then chilling, try to sleep, conserve energy, bail the boat, don't talk much, take another turn. On and on, through the night and then the day.

By which time Clancy Reece, Jon Barker and Craig Plummer would have done what Salmon River boatmen and river rangers swear to this day is impossible. In 24 hours, they'd have rowed from the eastern border of Idaho through its wild heart and nearly to its western edge. They'd have accordioned much of the nation's longest remaining freeflowing river into a one-day package using nothing but skill, will, and muscle.

Jon had tried to think of everything. The little-used Deer Gulch put-in had been chosen because what lay ahead through the hours of darkness was swift but easy water. The significant whitewater, with its potential for both greater speed and greater risk, would begin just after dawn.

On the drive upriver to their launch, Jon had studied the water that passed below and jotted notes about obstacles that might be dicey in darkness. Islands only passable on the left; bridge abutments only passable on the right; the cable car crossings that looked too low for safe clearance but weren't; the place where house-sized boulders clogged the main channel, leaving one safe route tight to the left bank.

Now the time for planning was done. They raced into night. Headlights began to trace the highway. Yard lights came on, transforming riverside houses into tableaux of shining ordinariness. Hillsides lost detail, became hulking shadows. For a while, the riverbank was still discernible by the glimmer of pale-trunked cottonwoods. Last to go, at 10 p.m., were the shining white wavetops. It was time to get out the spotlight.

They used the light sparingly, since one key question Jon had not considered in advance was how quickly the spot would deplete the car battery it had been wired to. They'd flick the light on, find the submerged log or the next bend or the fastest water, flick the light back off, and boat by feel and ear and memory.

Each time the light clicked off, the darkness was, for a few moments, complete. In those moments, Craig felt a visceral resistance to driving the fragile wooden shell of the dory forward into blackness. Not only could he not make himself do it, he could barely make himself sit there, one hand gripping the gunwale, and allow it to be done.

Jon and Clancy had boated in darkness before. They felt their senses spiral out, their whole bodies straining to replace information eyes could not provide. They also trusted what Craig at first could not. They knew that what their eyes told them when the light was on—that the path ahead was clear—would still be true with the light off. It got easier as their eyes began adjusting faster. Soon, even when the light was off, they could distinguish wavetops by their faint gather of starlight.

Less than an hour later, the dory swept around a corner and the spotlight's beam splashed against a massive logjam. The main force of the current flew at it, piled against it. They needed to dodge out of the current to the right. Clancy pivoted into a downstream ferry, stern pointing river right. This allowed him to maintain downstream speed while cutting diagonally across current.

After a half dozen strokes it was clear they weren't going to make it. The current was stronger than it had appeared, and now it was too late for the tactic a less confident oarsman might have chosen, an upstream ferry to slow the boat and buy maneuvering time.

"Row harder," warned Jon.

Clancy glanced over his shoulder and began to pull with oar-bending force, levering with his whole body. At the beginning of each stroke the dory surged as if goosed, but almost immediately current dampened the effort.

"Clarence—"

The logjam's hissing voice rushed in to surround them. There was a sickening crunch and the men tumbled forward. Clancy yanked on the upstream oar. The dory hesitated as if deciding whether to become a permanent part of the jam. Then it obeyed and spun away downstream. The hissing receded. Nobody spoke, but they were all aware that one of those moments had just passed, a moment in which normalcy becomes crisis and then flips back so fast it's hard to hang onto the significance of what has just happened.

Jon leaned out over the bow and felt something splintery and raw: a half-inch-wide, four-inch-long gash. He and Craig pulled gear out of the forward hold to survey the damage.

Water sloshed within the compartment, but luckily the hole was low. No more could enter than the eight or so inches already in, and since the forward compartment was otherwise still watertight, they wouldn't even have to bail the main seating area. Jon's good mood immediately returned. They didn't have to stop, he announced. They could repair the damage in the morning, perhaps even as they rowed.

More cautious now, the men concentrated on distinguishing general water sounds from the hiss of water pushing its way through underbrush, or the open-faucet sound it made pouring over rocks. They sought the center bead of current by instinct, and stayed in it by seeking even pressure against each oar blade, and by that steady, predictable rocking of the boat that only occurs on unconflicted water.

When the river was silent they heard the disgruntled cries of Canada geese disturbed by their passing. Night insects chorused. Occasionally there was a splash near shore, beaver perhaps, or muskrat. At other moments the stillness was so profound you could imagine you heard the tiny, isolated splash of a droplet from the muzzle of an unseen, drinking deer.

It was during one of those still moments that a vehicle on the highway pulled over. Moments later, a spotlight bright as their own shot out and glided downstream, then scanned more slowly back.

Finally it splashed onto the dory. For several seconds it followed them. Then it switched off. A state trooper, maybe? Craig told the others he saw the outline of a rack of emergency lights across the vehicle's roof. The men laughed, wondered aloud what the lawman had seen or heard that had made him light up the river, and what he'd thought when his beam found them. He probably figured they were idiots. Wasn't it great that no law existed to force them off the water? In the general merriment, Craig felt his sense of foreboding fade. His love of rivers and river adventures rose to the fore.

Occasional houses exuded a blue television glow. Inspired by the touch of the policeman's spotlight, the men began to flash their spot into these windows, a cryptic message from the night. Inside one house, shadowy figures scattered as though dodging gunfire. In another, pale faces swiveled to stare balefully over a couchback. The men laughed, filled with a fierce, lone wolf joy.

Time passed and now the increasingly rare houses were dark. Rowing was strenuous work and although the day had been warm, the night was not. Their own chilled sweat and the weight of darkness quieted them. At 1:44 a.m. by Jon's watch, the boat swept silently around a big righthand bend and into the town of Salmon, Idaho.

Salmon's main street crosses its namesake river on a bridge. Bluish street lights lit the water and showed the route between the pilings. The men switched off their spot so they could slip invisibly through. Headlights, voices and laughter drifted down from a late night party. It felt good to glide along, more a part of the river than of the human world above. A few minutes later, darkness surrounded them again and the town of Salmon was gone.

Several chilly, slow hours passed before light again reached across the water, this time neon red and white and sodium yellow. This was the rustic store, motel and restaurant called North Fork. The river had all night been paralleled by north-south Highway 93, the only major automobile route through the rugged mountains of east central Idaho. The highway continues north but to do so it must climb laboriously out of the Salmon River drainage, because at North Fork the river makes a sharp left.

The river above North Fork weaves through a broad valley, but here at this westward turning it begins to bore into the massive Idaho Batholith. This restricts its channel and allows the Salmon for the first time to show real muscle. This new incarnation of the river storms through wilderness, clear across Idaho in fact, until it reaches another obstacle, the resistant granite of the Seven Devils Mountains, which, like a wall, forces the river northward again toward its confluence with the Snake.

Before this day ended, Jon knew, they would see that northward turn. He thought, as he had so many times before, how a river could only be fathomed as an entirety that gave to and took its shape from the land; how his best projects had been, like the Source to Sea, at least partly a celebration of that greater wholeness; how here he was again with his old friend, challenging but also knowing, celebrating, demonstrating the uniqueness of this great river. On no other river he had ever heard of could so many miles be covered, motorless, in 24 hours. No other river had this volume, this gradient, for so many miles. And who else besides himself and Clarence would even think to harness those characteristics, much less actually undertake the challenge?

Exactly according to plan, the first hints of light found the men miles below North Fork on a mirror-smooth, slow stretch of river with low grassy banks, above the first real rapid, called Pine Creek. Even before light became warmth, the quarreling of birds and the return of detail to the hillsides brought an unreasoning lightheartedness. As though they had slept, the men felt refreshed and warmed, ready for the challenges ahead.

Seventeen

Racing the Day

As soon as they could see to effect repairs, the men eddied out. It was the first time they'd slowed for more than the seconds it took to switch oarsmen. Craig could see that halting the pellmell pace even for that necessary few minutes made Jon restless. What disconcerted Craig were the repairs themselves: a plywood patch screwed onto the hull from the outside, the hatch bailed and latched shut.

His good mood faded and the foreboding he'd felt off and on through the night crept back. A whitewater craft should hold air. It should be made of hypalon and, if it was damaged, patched with adhesive and more hypalon. That was your insurance. Almost no matter what went wrong with an inflated boat, it stayed at the surface where the air was. Before the trip, he'd offered to stuff the thwarts from his raft into the dory's side hatches and inflate them. The dory was fine as it was, he'd been told. Besides, they needed the hatch space.

If Craig had asked a few more questions, he might have heard what common sense should also have told him: Safety had not driven the choice of craft. Whitewater rafts are not only full of air, they are much more stable and easier to self-rescue onto after a flip than a dory. In almost every way, a raft would have made a better choice for a single-boat high water trip.

However, rafts are slow. Their flat floors mean that a great deal of surface area contacts a great deal of river. The bulbous noses slap waves instead of slicing into them. The best speed/safety compromise would have been a cataraft. These lightweight, double pontoon craft are more hydrodynamic than rafts and just as stable. But cat-boats were relatively new in the '90s and not yet familiar to old school boaters like Clancy and Jon.

Besides, all three wilderness whitewater speed records Jon and Clancy knew about had been set in dories, which many old timers thought of as 'real' boats, in exactly the way they thought of open oarlocks as a 'real' rowing setup.

Truth was, if safety was the first consideration Clancy's dory was exactly the wrong boat. But if safety was the first consideration this was also the wrong day, the wrong river, and the wrong plan, one solitary boat racing down a flooding maelstrom for hundreds of miles, negotiating dozens of rapids as fast as skill, strength, and current allowed, through cold night and hot day and what would certainly become judgment-clouding fatigue.

As the morning progressed and they began to hit bigger waves, the floor of the bow compartment often sloshed. Unlike most modern rafts and some dories, this area had not been constructed with a raised floor that could drain accumulated water. It had to be bailed by hand with the cut-up Clorox bottle Clancy had brought.

By this time, Craig had decided he would let these two do all the rowing if they liked it so much. He couldn't get the hang of those damned oarlocks. His awkwardness on the sticks created more risk when there was enough already. So Craig appointed himself head bailer. It wasn't much fun but it was fair. Every so often, as the dory sliced through a big wave, elegant as a raft can never be, he saw Clancy grin like a proud dad. It made the bailing a little less onerous.

Despite the rising heat of the June sun, Craig wore his drysuit zipped tight. He noticed that Jon wore his as well, although the man occasionally unzipped the big chest zipper in the flattest stretches. Clancy was still in his rainpants, hooded rainjacket and rubber irrigation boots over fleece long johns. Craig knew the getup was much more comfortable than a drysuit as the heat rose. It would be useless if Clancy swam but if Jon wasn't going to comment, Craig certainly wasn't. The neoprene wetsuit remained in the hatch. Nobody commented on that either.

When the river from time to time became more chaotic, Jon donned a second lifejacket and handed one to Craig. He had showed Craig how to rig a cam strap between his legs and through the jacket straps so the jacket couldn't be pulled off by even the most violent water. Jon didn't say anything when Clancy didn't put on his second jacket. Jon had been seeking out the biggest whitewater on several continents for almost two decades now. He'd seen water do things that made one lifejacket seem laughably inadequate. But Twerp was—well, he was Twerp. He knew the score. He'd earned the right to choose.

From here on there would be little opportunity to relax. During the night they had needed to be ready to highside into a bigger-than-usual wave, and one passenger always needed to be alert, spotlighting for the oarsman, but there had also been hours of near-sleep. Now flood-empowered wave trains rolled at them every few minutes. Some were as familiar as their names on Jon's map. Each of the men had seen these rapids many times, if at friendlier water levels. Others—the short-lived, monstrous children of the flood—would in a few weeks revert to ripples. Today they could capsize the dory.

Equally problematic was the flotsam washed along on this increasingly chaotic tide. The river corridor and all its tributaries were flushing themselves of a decade of accumulated deadfall and debris. Sixty-foot-long tree trunks barreled along, the most dangerous scraggled with branches and stubs that could capture an oar or punch through the dory's side. Every few minutes the men scanned the water. After a log was spotted, the spotter monitored until it was well behind them.

Even when there were no monster logs to deal with, there were still 'rafts,' jumbled masses of sticks and smaller logs. Their persistent tapping against the hull was disconcerting. Although these debris rafts presented no danger they did cause missed strokes.

The men avoided most of the big water, less for safety's sake than because breaking waves steal a boat's momentum. But because the goal was speed, many couldn't be avoided. The fastest current usually feeds the biggest waves. Every few minutes some unavoidable mountain of water broke on them, dumping hundreds of pounds of itself into the boat, to be bailed out by Craig, one Clorox bottleful at a time.

And so the quiet excitement of rowing through the night and the crystal clarity of early morning gradually faded into a monotonous string of powerful oar strokes, logs to be avoided, waves to be hit square, bailers full of water, truncated attempts to relax, and occasional tenuous moments when all that kept the boat from flipping were the fast reactions of three men hurling their bodies at a rising gunwale.

"That's 7.5 miles per hour since we passed North Fork," Jon would say. Or, "Ok it's 10:06. Hey, we were fast. That works out to almost 10.5 between the Middle Fork and Corn Creek."

Jon worked from a laminated sheet of landmarks and mileages he'd made. Clancy had great fun teasing him about this compulsive's tool, but each time they passed another of Jon's landmarks, especially if Clancy was rowing, the big man would grunt, "How fast?"

After they passed the mouth of the Middle Fork, the Salmon's largest tributary, Craig was unnerved to find that what he'd thought was an intimidating floodstage river all that morning had been tame. Suddenly the little dory was on a powerhouse of a river, complete with gravity-defying boils, waves easily taller than the boat was long, roaring holes that gulped down river debris, and huge eddies blanketed in undulating driftwood.

The boils were the most astounding feature of this new, shapelessly chaotic river. The men pointed them out, wondering aloud what the hell was happening beneath the surface to create those roiling hills, some of which were plenty big enough to knock the dory over.

The parade of waterborne wood stepped up dramatically too. The bow wave created by hard oarstrokes shoved most of the smaller pieces aside so they didn't hit the boat, but then fed them right under the oar blades.

Also more frequent were the trees. You didn't want to enter a rapid alongside one. In big waves a log could become a torpedo, a battering ram, sometimes even a semi-airborne javelin. The men could spot a large log from a couple hundred yards. The goal was always to pass it before the next rapid, so the straining oarsman would pull even harder, gasping with effort, until the spotter said they were safely ahead of the thing.

Usually, Craig thought, rivers had a manageable look. Even

a big rapid had a shape and predictability that made negotiating it feel like a dance. There were rules. But this was out of control. Craig was glad that the next time he saw this river it would be in its sane midsummer incarnation.

Jon entertained himself with a familiar train of thought. He noticed how the constant rowing, bailing, tree-dodging, and highsiding against near-flips conspired to compress time in a way which seemed almost to compress the river itself. This roiling, tumbling force, this timeless behemoth of a wilderness river, which had come into its full and awesome power for this handful of days, for the ninth time in 100 years, could be contained inside the confines of a single human day if he, Jon Barker, willed it so. And he did.

The men boated as conservatively as speed allowed. The goal was not to find the boat's limits, not to climb waves so big they rose like watery walls, not to slam through their foaming heads in a glorious buckling crash, a roar of wet and white and then it's done and you are blinking water from your eyes and howling in glee. And too damn bad it wasn't, thought Jon.

There was one rapid, however, that Jon knew they would have to gut. It was called Whiplash. In 1974, the record highwater year, a 28-foot motorized pontoon raft—similar to the craft Jon and Clancy used on their floodstage Lower Salmon Slide runs—had tried to sneak Whiplash. Its pilot had hoped to bypass the massive midstream curlers by using an eddy that edged the wavetrain. The trouble was that the eddy was a formidable obstacle in its own right. Inside it, currents zoomed and boiled. At the edge it shared with the downstream flow, huge whirlpools formed, spun themselves out, reformed. The pontoon boatman had hoped his boat's size, motor and momentum would ram him across the eddy line and then allow him to make way against the upstream force of the eddy. He never found out if that would have worked. As the big boat hit the eddy's near edge, it flipped.

Clancy's dory was nearly ten feet shorter and powered only by two oars. The thought of that rapid made Jon's heart speed, but he wasn't scared, not really. Listening to your fears only made sense when you might decide not to do a thing. A few days before the trip, Jon had talked at length with friend and longtime guide Frogg Stewart. Frogg had once taken a triple rig—three rafts lashed securely side-by-side—through Whiplash at around 100,000 cubic feet per second. Frogg carefully walked Jon through the moves as he remembered them. Jon had been running Whiplash in his head ever since.

Who should row it? Jon wanted to but when things got weird, Clarence's strength could sometimes salvage runs the smaller man could not. On the other hand, Jon had formed such a vivid mental picture of what it would look like, what he would do. Which was more critical, power or plan?

Whiplash is a quirky rapid. Formed by an S curve at a narrowing of the river channel, at lower flows it consists mostly of a tricky convergence of eddy lines. At high flows two violent eddies flank a thin road of downstream current that is visibly elevated above the leftside eddy, the eddy that had flipped that motorized 28 footer. That line of downstream current is stacked with waves as tall as a dory is long. They look intimidating, those waves, but the real problem is that the last in the series smashes like a trainwreck into the cliff wall that comprises the bottom curve of the S, creating a hill of exploding, aerated water. The current disappears into this mass. When it emerges, it bends suddenly left, spilling past a tremendous pit that looks like a whirlpool with teeth.

To run the rapid successfully at high flows, Frogg had told Jon, a boat must ride those big waves straight into the frightening pileup at the cliff wall. Then get deflected left, miss the pit, surf out just below and regain downstream current. The trick is to try to hit the wall, Frogg had said. You won't get there, but try. Try real hard.

If you didn't stay on the raised line of current, you'd flip on the eddy line. Not a nice swim. But if you didn't plow far enough into that monstrous cliffside boil, you'd flip at its lip, or you'd get surfed into the weird pit. The swim that would follow that mistake was better not dwelt upon. Come to think of it, bad swim, good swim, what did it matter to Jon, Clancy and Craig? This was a one-boat trip. Even 'safe' swims would be tremendously risky. If they flipped, or if one of them simply got swept out and washed beyond a rescue rope's reach, there was no backup. All problems had to be solved by the three men present, with the gear they had at hand, or not solved at all.

Jon decided he wanted to row. Hitting the boil was a strength move, but the key to this rapid, according to Frogg, was hitting it exactly in the right spot. Jon's picture of the rapid was by now so clear it felt like he'd run it already. Besides, this was his trip, or more his than anyone else's. If something were to go wrong it would most likely happen here. The weight of that should fall on him.

Clancy agreed. It's not Jon's way to wonder at others' thoughts, but if he had, the younger man might have felt proud: Clancy trusted nobody as well as himself. Certainly the man remembered the too-energetic boy he had helped contain and later train. Yet at that critical moment, he was willing to ride—and let his beloved boat ride—in the hands of the man that wild boy had become.

So Jon had the oars as they swept around the last bend above the rapid. He spun the boat forward to set up his line and saw, at the end of the wavetrain, that massive boil, as big and violent as Frogg had said. He could see why that pontoon boat had wanted to avoid it. Looking at the turbulence of the eddy line, he could see why it had failed.

He also saw a rafting party, only the second they'd passed.

Because that was the river's other transformation. Usually busy with boaters seeking this river's rare combination of exciting whitewater and weeklong, wilderness length, the Salmon had so far been nearly deserted. This other party had tied their boats ashore above the rapid. They must be scouting. A good idea, but against the rules of the speed run.

In the few seconds remaining to him, Jon studied the water. He saw how the waves on that raised line of current, big as they were, were clean and faced straight on. They would be no problem. He angled a hair further right. He meant to stay well away from that left eddy.

Then they were in the waves. Jon lost sight of his target in each trough, saw it again as he topped each wave. Three waves remaining, then two, then one and they were there, rushing down the steep back of the last wave, Jon setting the oars, lined up just right, he thought, pushing hard, pushing onto—no, more like *into*—the frothing pile. The dory hit hard, stuck a moment, Clancy and Craig highsiding the bucking right side, Jon straining forward on the oars and then, just as it should, the boat began to sunfish, heeling left with its bow high. What wasn't as it should be was that immense pit. It was at Jon's left hip. It needed to be at his stern. He hadn't pushed far enough in. He poured all his strength into the oars and, as the dory finished its pivot, it shifted forward. They dropped off the boil just beyond that huge mouth.

Before Jon could congratulate himself, something weird happened. They had lost their forward momentum to the boil. Now they fell into some kind of seam. All around them currents rushed, roaring this way and that beneath them while, weirdly motionless, they surfed in place.

Don't move, they told each other tensely, don't move! Each man dropped low, trying to center his weight. Be careful. Keep 'er flat.

Jon feathered his oars gingerly into the rushing water. If he did anything wrong here and maybe even if he didn't, they'd be swimming almost before they felt the flip begin.

But they didn't flip. As suddenly as they'd been dropped into that frozen moment, it released them back into current, back into ordinary waves and out the bottom of the rapid. Upright, with Whiplash behind them.

There was an instant of silence and then Craig and Clancy began howling. The people on shore howled back and then Jon was howling, too. The men rolled down the tailwaves in a sloshing wooden bathtub, in water cold enough to numb exposed skin, heads thrown back, roaring with glee.

Jon quickly collected himself, spun the boat and began again to pull hard downstream. Craig began bailing. God, isn't that living? they told each other. That's what it's all about. Have you ever taken a hit that hard? Can you believe we made it? I thought we were over. It could have gone either way, you know it's true. Imagine what a swim in that right eddy would be like? Yah well, how about the left? Wonder what that other group thought of our run?

They would later learn that the other group thought they were nuts. The party had indeed pulled over to scout but, after studying the water, had decided to spend the rest of the day portaging their boats down the shore.

Quiet returned to the boat and with it, for Jon, a renewed awareness of how much the river had grown, and how dramatically it was about to grow again just a few miles downstream.

He'd reveled as each side creek boiled into the Salmon, some brown, some crystal-white and frothy, all exploding over their banks. Through the night and much of the day, he'd let his mind play with numbers. The 10,000 or so cubic feet per second they'd launched into at Deer Gulch had doubled and doubled and was in the process of doubling again. He drew the river map in his head. He knew that soon they'd enter a short reach, 17 miles long, into which, bam!, the South Fork and four other major creeks pump much of the runoff of the Gospel Hump Wilderness directly into the mainstem Salmon.

With each overflowing creek, the river had morphed a little. How much would it transform in those short miles below the South Fork, with all that additional water slamming in? Since they'd passed the Middle Fork at midmorning, he'd been seeing the kind of high-water strangeness, the weirdly surging eddies and oversized waves, that he could never get enough of. Now those boils and surges and waves and turbulent eddies were growing. And surely would grow more below the South Fork. He couldn't wait to see.

Craig bailed with increasing fatigue. It was hot. They'd been on the water, he suddenly realized, more than 17 hours. Because of Jon's regular announcements, he knew they were averaging nine miles per hour, had traveled more than 150 miles. The thought of all those miles behind and yet so many still ahead felt as heavy as a boatload of water.

There were few rapids now, which meant there was little to distract him from the desire for sleep. And yet Craig couldn't sleep, couldn't even relax. At other flows this low-gradient section was unchallenging, to say the least—some call it Salmon Lake—but now currents heaved themselves back and forth like whales rolling just beneath the surface, and eddies surged out and grabbed at the dory. He found himself highsiding almost as much in this supposed flatwater as he had in the rapids upstream. Except the chore had become more tedious than exhilarating.

Craig continued to man the bailer. It was the least he could do. He wondered how the other two could keep up that steady, hard rowing pace in such an uncooperative craft on such a heaving flood. He liked the doing/overdoing joke, but to him that was what it was, a joke, not a damned mantra.

But those two? They behaved exactly as they had at 9 p.m. the previous night. They had to be tired. Craig was and for most of the trip he hadn't even rowed. Between them, he figured, they had like 50 years more river experience than he did, but that didn't exempt them from exhaustion.

Or maybe it did. Maybe they were as unlike happy-go-lucky Craig Plummer as they seemed. Jon probably was, with that intense focus of his, the way he seemed to listen to you but was really tuned to his own private radio. Craig could almost believe that Jon felt nothing but desire to reach his goal, and that that desire had neither grown nor faded since the trip began. Maybe it never did, just redirected itself to the next goal, and then the next. Exhausted? The guy had to be. But maybe he didn't know it.

Clancy was more like a regular guy, more soft-spoken than most but funny as hell. He liked to party. He clearly loved his dory. But he also contained a massive, muscular power that seemed every bit the match to Jon's inflexible will. Clancy was not a young man and packed some extra pounds for sure, but still he seemed like Hercules or something. The more tired Craig became, the more he felt out of his league, stuck on an adventure that wouldn't end with a superhero and a mastermind.

And so the last miles stacked up, Jon occasionally calling out their time and speed. The last of the pizza was eaten, the water and chocolate milk drunk. Jon rowed, throwing his body backward with the effort. Then Clancy, who as his turn was ending always grunted the same question: How fast?

Jon rowed again. Then Clancy. The men highsided. Craig bailed. Bailed again. Scoop after scoop of river water, eight pounds a gallon, flesh-brown and, at 48 degrees, cold as hell.

The river was almost as big now as it was going to get. Only a few miles remained until they reached the last rapid that counted. It was called Chittam. It had a good sneak, a route that allowed a boat to avoid its biggest whitewater. If they missed that line Chittam would take them on a wilder ride than Whiplash had, but below Chittam the wilderness ended and a road reached upriver from Riggins. Roads meant people and people meant security. Besides, Clancy knew the water down there so well from his Salmon River Challenge daytrip days he could probably run it in his sleep. There were big rapids downstream, but Clancy was the guy who, once upon a time, had figured out how to safely run commercial trips through the biggest of those rapids. When Chittam was behind them, this trip would be in the bag.

In the surging, eddy-woven miles before the wilderness boundary, Clancy said he wanted to row. The muscles of his forearms burning, Jon surrendered the rowing seat to his old friend. It was 5:30 p.m. They had been on the water for almost 21 hours.

For the last time in his 27 year whitewater career, Clancy Reece bent his back against the oars.

Eighteen

Disaster

A hissing roar rolled toward the men from below a distinct horizon line, beyond which the river seemed to disappear. Chittam.

If a camera could have panned over that lip that day in 1996, it would have recorded a maelstrom. The rapid was on a tight righthand bend. Above the turn the river dropped fast and smooth, gathering speed. When that speeding water encountered the left-bank cliff the rapid exploded. Friction pushed up massive lateral waves, too big to run, on the left. On the right, trashy holes and waves blocked an easy sneak.

The strategy for Chittam was opposite the one for Whiplash. In Whiplash, the only possible route had driven straight into the heart of the rapid. In Chittam, Clancy had to begin the same way, on the smooth, V-shaped tongue that fed the rapid's heart. But that was only to borrow speed from the water. The trick in Chittam was to make a well-timed escape to the right just before the V's apex. If his timing was perfect, they'd slide bone-dry between two big waves and be done.

Clancy knew the run by heart. As the water began to accelerate, he angled stern first for maximum rowing power. Then he raised his oars from the water and waited.

The roar reached out to enfold them while the boat still ran on glossy brown water. No matter how many times you experienced that powerful acceleration down the V of a big rapid, the speed gathered faster than you expected. And always there was that breathless anticipation.

Oars hovering, Clancy waited. Waited past the moment Jon would have started, then past the moment Jon began to wish he would start, and a little longer yet. Then the oars dropped. Three fast, oar-bending strokes and the stern had pierced the right edge of the V. The dory slipped across the trough of a wave so smooth and deep that for a moment Jon could see nothing but the wall of water before them and a matching wall behind. An instant later, the first massive lateral devoured the V's point, but the dory wasn't there anymore. The thing was done.

Clancy swung the boat to face the line of giant laterals they had escaped. These were nothing like the clean haystacks between which he'd just slipped. They surged and collapsed and rose again like living things, like roaring, deep-troughed monsters feeding off that cliff wall. They were bigger than anything the men would see once the water dropped and the guiding season began. Which didn't matter because you couldn't run waves like that with guests on your boat. They'd agreed it wasn't a good idea on this trip, either: Not only would the necessary bailing afterward slow them, but adding unnecessary risk on a one-boat trip wasn't smart.

Clarence's boat angle told Jon there might be a change of plan on this, the biggest remaining rapid of their adventure. He glanced back. Clarence was wearing a tiny grin Jon knew well. His heart quickened. He grinned back. When the big man began laughing low in his belly, Jon spun forward, hunkered low in the nose.

"Hang on," he told Craig.

And the dory surged forward hard, slipped across the shoulder of one monster wave, dropped straight into the trough of the next and swiveled to face the thing full-on.

Whitewater boaters tend to divide themselves into categories. There are creek boaters who run steep, tight water. Their style of boating takes finesse but also a willingness to scrape rocks and free-fall or "huck" over the lips of waterfalls. There are play boaters who perform gymnastic tricks on waves and in holes. Jon and Clancy were of a third category, big water boaters. Jon in particular had traveled the world looking for bigger and bigger whitewater. What big water boaters relish is the chance to face off against watery mountains.

So, suddenly facing a wall, no, an overhung cliff of upended river, Jon was not worried—he was impressed. And intensely curious to see how Clarence would manage. Because this wave was *huge*. He himself would not have run it. Hell, he wasn't positive he could.

Then the wave toppled onto the boat. So did the next. And the next. Jon was blinded, buried in white. By feel, he threw his body forward as the bow dropped into each trough, using his weight to help Clancy drive toward the next wave. Each breaking wave captured the dory for an instant, but the boat never bobbled. It sliced through the crest and down the huge wave-back toward the next hit.

And then they were through. Jon was filled with joy and

something like gratitude. Clancy had put the perfect finish to a perfect trip. He turned back into his friend's grin. He felt like he might burst, but he knew his part. "Nice job," was all he said.

"Boat handles pretty good," the big man replied.

Now well below the rapid, they were being shuttled river-right by a strange, hard current, as though on a conveyor. It bore them through the turbulence at the bottom of the rapid. On the left bank, across the rapidly widening water gap, was the Vinegar Creek boat ramp, its parking lot mostly empty, no people in sight. Civilization regained. End of wilderness.

But they weren't out of the water yet. Literally. Icy river filled the boat to just inches below the gunwales. The men sat thigh-deep. Small waves lapped in and, as the water inside shifted one way and another, so, drunkenly, did the dory. There was no jumping and howling as after Whiplash. The dory was simply too unstable, too full of water, the currents too powerfully discordant. They needed to get to shore and bail.

Which was fortunate because like it or not, that odd current was driving them toward the right bank. Jon grabbed the bowline and eased to the nose, keeping his weight low. Clancy pushed forward across a surging eddy line. The boat wallowed, then steadied. They were in. But as they neared the bank, Jon noticed a big log just offshore. At best it would make landing awkward. At worst it could damage the dory. He looked downstream at the next eddy, thirty or so yards off, and back at the log. One end of it suddenly heaved two feet upward and then subsided.

"Let's go for the next cove," said Jon, simultaneously reaching with one Converse-clad foot to push the boat back into current.

Clancy took a few strokes, letting the dory drift downstream toward the next eddy. Jon waited in the nose with the bowline.

Moments later, a boil rose beneath their right side and grabbed

162

the gunwale and, with startling implacability, began to roll the dory. The men threw themselves left against the rise, but the right gunwale had already slipped below the river's surface. River inside met river outside and, in slow motion, poured them out. The boat finished upside down, black hull facing the sky.

Jon would later replay those moments obsessively. What nagged at him, although he didn't consciously register it at first, was his friend's behavior. There was nothing wrong exactly, except that Clarence didn't act like Clarence. The big man should have been surging forward, singlehandedly righting the boat, playing his usual laconic Superman. They'd rigged a flip line at the put-in. All during the trip it had waited, stretched beneath the boat from oarlock to oarlock, a nylon insurance policy. Now they simply had to reach high on that rope, brace against the hull and pull together, hard. But Clarence merely bobbed in the water, grasping the gunwale as though something interesting had just occurred to him and he couldn't be bothered until he'd puzzled it through.

Jon slipped into his friend's role, telling Clarence and Craig to grab the flipline, counting one-two-three-pull!

The boat rolled soggily upright, even more awash than before. Shore was only twenty feet off as the men, one at a time, crawled delicately back aboard. Clarence wordlessly returned to the oarsman's seat. Again, Jon would later wonder at himself. Why didn't he note his friend's disinterested silence? If he had, would the events of the next hours have unraveled differently?

Jon again moved to the nose with the bowline. What he expected was that Clarence would ease them back to shore at the next eddy. They would bail and be off.

What happened was this: The river bellied again, or it opened up, or it sucked at them, whatever, and the water inside the dory lunged in sympathy and rolled the three men back into the dark, cold river.

Nineteen

Tunnel Vision

Craig Plummer surfaced, grabbing the gunwale. He was as frightened as he could remember ever being. He couldn't see Jon or Clancy, didn't know what they were doing, but he was pretty sure it didn't matter. Even if they could right the dory, it had no bailing bucket. He'd seen that when they rolled it up the first time. He thought he'd seen one oar gone, too, along with the spare. Upside down, the thing floated low, perhaps two foot above water. It would be just as bad rightside up until they got the water out which, without a bailer, they couldn't. Unless they could get it to shore which, if he was right about the missing oars, they couldn't.

From the start, this trip had felt precarious to Craig. Suddenly he understood why: For the last 20 hours, they'd never been more than an instant from this. The river had gotten inside and now the dory was useless as driftwood. And without a boat, Craig reasoned frantically, wasn't it every man for himself?

He struck for the left bank and the road, swimming hard. But the water surprised him with what felt like a furious, living resistance. It pushed and grabbed, and no matter how hard he swam, if it pushed backward, backward he went. He had swum whitewater before, but never in flood. And never had he set out to swim nearly the entire width of a big river. His previous swims had lasted only as long as it took to right a flipped raft. Now as the minutes passed and he was shuttled this way and that by the river like a mouse between a cat's paws, he began to doubt his decision to abandon ship.

He swam more slowly, tried to calm himself and think. His two lifejackets floated him reassuringly high. His drysuit kept him warm, at least for now. Maybe he should go back. Those two were probably trying to save the dory. He could help them. They could all help each other. He turned to try to see Clancy and Jon through the huge rolls of water. But what he glimpsed when he crested his next wave made no sense: Jon, crouched atop the dory, doggedly trying to flip it. Alone.

Then he saw Clancy. The big man floated between Craig and Jon. He wasn't swimming, just bobbing among debris from the boat—dry bags, paco pads, his own second lifejacket.

Clancy was staring at him. It took a moment to decipher the expression Craig read on the heavy face. It took another moment to believe it. Because what Craig thought he saw was fear. Hopeless, blank-eyed, animal fear. *Clancy?* Oh god, this must really be bad.

Now Jon was staring at Craig too, was yelling at him, but Craig, shocked and confused by Clancy's expression, couldn't make heads or tails of Jon's words. A funny, irrelevant thought popped into his head: Jon looked like an ant being swept downstream on a stick. Swim for shore, Craig silently urged them both, swim! Because that's damn sure what I'm going to do.

He turned toward the distant shore and its road, again swimming hard, again fighting panic. When he began to tire he forced himself to slow his strokes and conserve strength. An inflatable sleeping pad floated by, unrolled, and he grabbed it for the extra flotation, although it made swimming even less effective. What did that matter? The river was in charge. What Craig would do was keep swimming and try to stay calm.

Jon came up fast after the second flip and grabbed the boat. They were in downstream current. Shore moved past with increasing speed. Damn.

He looked for Clarence and was startled at what he saw. The first rule of river carnage says that even upside down, your boat is your most important asset. It's bigger, sturdier, and floats higher than you. If you can, you grab hold. But Clarence floated an arm's length from the gunwale, motionless, as though unaware that there was a boat anywhere near. The current hadn't pulled him away yet but any moment it would. And there was something about his face, something that made Jon blurt the unthinkable: "Twerp, do you want to take my hand?"

The man turned his head.

"Y-e-s," he said, stretching the word into its component sounds.

Jon gripped Clarence by one wrist, maintaining his firm hold on the boat with his other hand. Clarence wrapped his hand around Jon's wrist too, but his grip felt like an infirm old man's when it should have crushed Jon's forearm. That weak grip, even more than the odd expression and the way he had spoken, slammed into Jon's heart like an avalanche. Something was wrong. Jon grabbed for the flipline and pulled experimentally, rocking the dory only a little. No, he couldn't hold Clarence *and* flip the boat. And he knew, suddenly, urgently, that he couldn't let go of Clarence.

An odd tunnel vision kicked in. All that mattered was that Clarence was in trouble. It didn't matter what Craig was doing because he wasn't close enough to be a resource. It didn't matter what was happening inside Clarence's body. Hypothermia, a blow to the head the first time they flipped, a heart attack, a stroke—Jon's job was the same no matter what. Get his friend out of the water.

They were in tangled currents that yanked at Jon's legs and tried to haul Clarence from him. Waves raised the boat above their heads, dropped it an arm's length beneath them. It took most of his concentration simply to hang onto both the boat and his friend. But Jon knew he had an even bigger problem. Somewhere just downstream was Vinegar Rapid, likely washed out except for one nasty hole, but that hole was big enough to swallow this dory and powerful enough not to spit it out. It was on river right. So were they.

Jon had positioned himself near the nose of the boat with Clarence before him. Twerp's downstream view was unimpeded, but Jon was almost positive the man saw nothing. Getting them both through this was Jon's job alone.

He could see past the big man's head that the hole was still out of sight around a bend, but he was pretty sure they were on track to hit it. He began kicking hard toward the left shore. As they passed the last couple of cars in the Vinegar Creek parking lot, he risked stopping long enough to yell for help. He didn't expect a reply and didn't get one. Even if someone had been there, river noise would probably have masked Jon's cries.

He could see Craig now, occasionally, as waves lifted one man or the other. Craig was upstream, further left, and swimming hard. He would miss the hole. Fine. Jon could ignore him. He began again to kick.

"We've got to swim left, Twerp. Hang on," he said. Clarence still held Jon by the wrist. With his other hand, to Jon's relief, he finally reached for the nose of the boat. Jon thought Clarence was even kicking a little. That was good, because now he heard a roaring ahead.

"We're coming to the hole. Hang onto me. It'll be smoother after that."

As the roar reached toward them, Jon made hard scissor kicks whenever the turbulence allowed. Other times it tangled his legs and dragged at him, and all he could do was hold onto his friend and the dory. Immediately ahead he saw a boiling hill of water, behind which, he knew, lay a giant, submerged boulder. Below that boulder was the hole.

"It looks good, Twerp. Here we go. Hang on," he yelled over the swelling noise, and concentrated on maintaining his twin grips.

The men swirled toward the bulge, Jon still kicking but now also sucking lungfuls of air, ready to take his last breath just as they crested, hoping Clarence understood well enough what was about to happen to do the same. If the crest of the bulge didn't deflect them as he hoped, they'd drop into that hole. Their lifejackets would mean nothing. They would tumble down and down until up was an abstraction and shrinking lungfuls of air were the only things that mattered in the whole world.

Their speed increased and at first they seemed to be aimed directly at the hole, but Jon had been right: The current that contained them split like a bow wave. Their half bent left, sped past the submerged boulder with feet to spare, then past the gaping mouth of the hole.

Jon didn't dwell on the victory. He needed to get Clarence out of the water. That meant righting the boat. But he needed Clarence's help to right the boat and he was almost certain it would not be forthcoming. Getting that dory rightside up was so critical Jon could almost feel oars in his hands, feel the power and control conferred by 10 feet of leverage extending from each arm.

Meanwhile the current smoothed, whisked them 10, 20, 30 feet below the hole, then dumped them into a chaotic spin of cross-currents. Which pulled the two men apart as easily as if their arms were made of wet newspaper. Within moments, Twerp was lost to sight among the three-foot waves.

Everything was still fixable, Jon told himself. He had to stay focused was all. Somehow, because it had to happen, he *would* flip the dory. Flip it, ease himself inside, use one of the extra plastic jugs in the cooler as a bailer if necessary, then get his hands on those oars and row over to pick up first Clarence and then Craig.

Jon crawled onto the black hull, braced his feet against the chine, reached as high as he could on the flip line and hauled back. The boat shifted soggily but did not come upright. Perhaps a hatch had blown open and was scooping water. Perhaps the woven turbulence of the flood interfered, pinching the craft between opposing currents. He would pull harder. He let the boat back down, braced, reached high and then lunged backward with all his weight. The boat came almost perpendicular to the water, but then it again stuck fast. Jon let himself fall awkwardly onto his forearms and knees and the dory slipped back into its original position. On his next attempt he leaned off the upstream side, letting the current push with him against the hull as he pulled. Maybe it tipped a little further—Jon's feet felt braced against a vertical surface—but it stuck just as adamantly. He released the boat, fell onto the hull, rose to try again. And, more urgently, again.

And then it was time to face facts: An upright boat was his best chance to salvage everything, but he wasn't getting the goddamn job done. From atop the rocking hull, he could see Clarence perhaps

150 feet upstream. Jon made himself study the man carefully, calmly. His head was out of the water, but was he still conscious? Jon realized with a chill that he wasn't sure.

What was happening here? True, Clarence wasn't wearing a drysuit as both he and Craig were, and the water was bitterly cold. But it had been ten minutes, tops, since the man had grinned at him in Chittam, clearly in jubilant control of mind and body. Hypothermia, a dangerous loss of core temperature that gradually steals physical and mental acuity and finally kills, couldn't work that fast, could it?

Jon didn't think so but he wasn't sure. The fact that he was warm didn't mean Clarence wasn't dangerously cold. The river had direct contact only with Jon's hands and head. Twerp's cheap raingear offered no real protection. He might as well be taking a bath in the cold water. On the other hand, Clarence had been acting strangely since the first flip. Whatever was happening to his friend, Jon was suddenly positive time was running out.

Jon spotted Craig further upstream. The man had stopped swimming and was looking back at them. Good.

"Swim over," he yelled, waving Craig in. "Swim over!"

If Craig helped Clarence, made sure his face stayed out of the water, Jon could keep trying to flip the boat, maybe think of a more effective way, maybe milk more power out of his body. If necessary Craig could leave Clarence just long enough to help. Everything could still be OK.

Craig seemed to hear Jon over the shouting of the flood. He stared across the waves. Stared for what seemed a long time, first at Jon and then at Clarence. Then he suddenly turned to swim away.

Jon was running out of options. He was relatively safe on the boat, safe from powerful hydraulics, from the tremendous amount of waterborne wood, from eventual exhaustion and hypothermia. He could stay aboard until the boat swung close to an eddy he could leap for, or until someone saw him from shore. For him, this whole thing was all but over—as long as he stayed on the hull.

Through a decade of adventures he and Clarence had watched each other's backs, each trusting that they were in turn watched. That trust had never been tested. Now it was, and so far Jon was failing.

Jon studied his friend again. The big man's eyes appeared closed. His head slumped forward. His face almost touched water. Twerp was out of time.

You never go back in, Jon thought as he cinched his lifejacket straps tighter. This river is in flood. It's strange and it's dangerous. You don't go back in because the first rule of rescue is that rescuers do not allow themselves to become victims. And that's what anybody floating in this river right now is, a victim.

Jon Barker snatched Clarence's extra lifejacket from where it nudged against the boat, slipped an arm into it, took a deep breath, and jumped. Dunked, broke surface, and began swimming hard for his friend.

Craig felt a rude shove from behind. His face plunged forward. He flailed, surfaced, reached back and felt wood. It was a by-god tree, massive root ball and all, headed downriver roots first. The thing was maybe 50 feet long, the broken-off remnant of a massive ponderosa. The root ball, still pushing at him although now he held it off with both hands, was the size of a Volkswagen.

Now Craig had a new fear. This tree could easily become a projectile in the powerful currents. He told himself he had to get away from it and fast, but instead he found himself clutching the thing. After a few minutes it occurred to him that its bulk might shield him from other blows. He knew from keeping watch in the dory all day that this tree was one of many. How had he forgotten? He looked around wildly and realized that yes, he was surrounded by chunks and branches and even other trees. They were everywhere.

But his tree would stay in the main current. It would not go to shore. He made himself push away from it and begin to swim as he had right after leaving the dory, a hard, fast crawl. He might as well have been attempting to swim straight up into the air. The river shuttled him where it wanted, which was a little right and then a little left but never near shore.

Again he felt panic rise. He gave himself a hard mental shake, told himself to stop thinking about what it would be like to die out here.

He began making himself count strokes. Kick-and-stroke, kick-and-stroke, kick-and-stroke. At 100 he looked up. No progress. Next he counted to 150. No progress. He looked downstream to a point of land, behind which would be an eddy. The current arced within a tantalizing 50 feet of that point of land. His heart thumped. He swam harder. Fifty feet was all he had to make. Maybe 100 strokes? But when he next looked up, in his urgency having lost count, he was passing the jut of land. It wasn't 50 feet away. It was now at least 50 yards off, and growing more distant as he stared.

Ok, he told himself, grateful that at least he was too tired for panic, if the river wanted him ashore, it would take him there. If it didn't, well, he wouldn't think about that. He, Craig Plummer, would swim and swim and swim, whether it made any difference or not, because swimming was better than thinking. Because if he stopped swimming he *would* panic despite the exhausted weight of his arms. He thought he knew how that story ended.

Time passed. There were no rapids, but the flooding river was far from calm. Logs and sticks jostled him, current swirled and spun him, boils pushed and pulled at him. No other trees ambushed him although several passed near. He quickly grew too tired for an aggressive crawl, especially wearing two lifejackets. He rolled onto his back. He was too tired to swim but he kept swimming. He did not look toward shore.

More time passed, and then he felt an almost playful tumble of crosscurrents that slowed his speed. He realized he must have contacted an eddy line, and not a monstrous one but a small, safe one. He was vaguely surprised at his response, which was not relief but a powerful fear that if he let himself believe the ordeal might be over, it wouldn't be. He did not pick up his head to look, just kept up those steady, exhausted backstrokes. Now he thought he might be drifting upstream. If that were true, he really was safe, really was in a calm little eddy. He rolled over then and saw before him twiggy shrubs. His hands grabbed and caught, and then he was holding onto shore.

He wasn't going to die. The thought sank slowly through him until it landed in the pit of his stomach. He pulled himself further up the eddy, hand over hand, weak as a fevered child. Then he crawled out on his knees, rose, stumbled up onto the road, bent double and puked fear and relief out onto the dirt.

He thought, vaguely, that he should be cold after a swim of what, thirty minutes maybe? But all he felt was watery exhaustion. Thank god for drysuits. He pulled the top half over his head and knotted its arms around his waist, dry heaved a few more times, and began walking down the road. Somewhere downriver was the little town of Riggins. Between here and there he would find Jon and Clancy. That is, he thought with a jangle of alarm strong enough to shatter his stupor, if they were still alive.

Jon was pretty sure he and Clarence had been in the water

together this second time, after he abandoned the dory, for at least 20 minutes. He couldn't quite make sense of the fact that they were still in the middle of the river. It didn't seem possible that, with absolutely everything at stake, he couldn't swim them in.

When he'd reached Clarence, he'd been pretty sure his friend was not breathing. Jon had attempted rescue breathing, but the downward pressure it took to get a good seal around their mouths had pushed them both beneath the water. He'd reached beneath Clarence's arms, cinched the lifejacket tight, tried again. No good.

Since then, he'd been attempting to swim the unconscious man to shore. Cold could help as well as hurt, Jon knew. Cold slowed the metabolism, decreased the body's need for oxygen. If only he could reach shore, even after all these precious minutes had ticked away, he might yet buy his friend a fighting chance.

But the man's limp bulk was like a sea anchor, like the drogue he'd taught Jon those wind-buffeted days on the Columbia. No matter how hard Jon swam, he never managed to get more than 15 or 20 feet from the center bead of the current. Eddy after eddy swept by, minutes devoured themselves, and although Jon didn't feel fatigued, he knew he couldn't keep this up forever.

By now, the river had been pinched into a sheer canyon, its restricted waters relatively smooth at the surface but tremendously turbulent beneath. Currents grabbed at his feet with surprising force, shoved and punched at him, yanked at Clarence.

Then, from a violent eddy line yards away, a boil surged toward them and the men were suddenly beneath the river's skin. Darkness. Jon tried to relax and focus only on keeping hold of Clarence. When the river released them, Jon's extra lifejackets brought him up first. Coughing, he hauled at the heavier man until his lolling head broke the surface.

Jon pulled Clarence's limp bulk close. He braced against the big man's chest and yanked the straps even tighter, not letting himself think about why he was doing this. Then he grabbed the shoulder of his friend's jacket and redoubled his efforts to swim them in.

The canyon had narrowed still further and the increased turbulence was evident in violent eddy lines and incredible boils. Jon watched for turbulence he thought could take them down. If he was mistaken and Clarence was still breathing, the man's face must at all costs stay above the surface.

Five minutes later, at an eddy line that looked like a dozen they had floated through without mishap, the river took them again. Let them up. A time later, it took them again. This time Jon felt the pull intensify rather than weaken as they dropped. Five, ten feet beneath the surface, in pounding darkness, Clarence somewhere below, pulling Jon down and down.

A.K. and Maryé Barker dropped off of Whitebird Pass onto the Salmon River, headed upstream toward Riggins. Hoping to surprise Clarence and their son, they had driven from Lewiston with A.K.'s lifejacket, a box of cookies and a long rope. If Clarence and Jon could be convinced to pull over—a big if, the couple knew, since speed was the point of this trip—A.K. would hop in and run the final miles with them. If the boat would not pull over, the two planned to lower the cookies from one of several bridges near Riggins. They knew their son. There was probably nothing entertaining to eat on that boat, if there was any food at all.

When they reached the little town of Lucile, they dropped in at a rafting company called Northwest Voyageurs to ask the guides if they'd seen Jon and Clarence. None had. They continued upriver, scanning the water for Clarence's familiar dory.

They passed Riggins, left pavement and continued upriver.

They were high on the Salmon River Road, perhaps 12 miles from road's end at Vinegar Creek, when they saw a boat floating upside down in midstream. The black hull was unmistakeable: Clarence had worked on his dory all spring in the Barker warehouse.

Maryé was alarmed, A.K. calm. Boats flip in big water, he reminded her. That's what lifejackets are for. We'll go pick them up, then figure out what to do about the dory.

A few minutes later they saw a flash of red across the river, just above the waterline. Maryé's eyes went wide at the sight of Jon's drysuit. Without thermal protection in that cold water, lifejacket or not, he could die.

A.K. looked hard. The suit was too far above the water and too neatly laid out to have been washed there. No, he told his wife. That suit is good news: It means he's not in the river. It means they're OK. Jon has left that suit there for a signal. He wants people to see it.

Less than a half-mile back, they'd passed a private cable car crossing. That drysuit had been on the far, roadless side of the river. Jon and Clarence would not stay on the roadless side and they certainly wouldn't attempt to swim for the road, not without drysuits. Clearly then, they would try to cross on the cable. A.K. turned the car around.

Far below the river's surface, yanked downward by one arm, Twerp invisible in the darkness below, Jon felt his grip slipping. Or felt himself letting go, he wasn't sure which. The need to breathe rose in him like a command and then his fingers were empty. Instantly he began rising. Then he was sucking chestfuls of air, alone.

Seconds later Clarence's body came up in a slower skein of current. Jon stared. Already the gap between them was 30 feet. Then it was 40, then 50. He could probably still get back. But he made no move. The decision had been made down there in the dark, hadn't it? Get back and what? Float downstream with the body of your dead friend, dragged again and again into airless cold by his limp weight, on and on into the night? The moment he had been fighting to save himself from, even after he'd stopped believing he could save Twerp, was suddenly on him.

But how to actually do it? How do you abandon your partner, even if you believe your partner has already abandoned you? The expanse of water stretched between them as Jon struggled for something to say or do or think that would make this moment bearable. Because it really, really was not. Finally he raised his hand as though to wave or perhaps salute, heard himself say, "Bye, Twerp."

He knew Clarence couldn't hear him. Nor did it help him do what he had to do. He said it again anyway.

It didn't help that time, either.

And then Jon completed his unbearable act, turning alone toward shore.

He'd never imagined he could fail when success was so critical. Now, in a few minutes, he'd be standing, alone, on shore. Clarence's body would float on, far more alone, down their beloved Salmon River. Jon could still feel the pressure on the sole of his foot as he'd pushed the dory back from the unstable log below Chittam, opting, he thought, for a calmer eddy below. That unremarkable snap decision had held the seeds of every moment since, including this one. It boggled his mind that a tiny act like a foot pushing away from a log—so easy to do or not do—had made inevitable everything that had happened since.

Thoughts like that could incapacitate a man. Jon shoved them away. He picked the first big eddy that arced toward him. He let go of the extra lifejacket which had helped return him to the surface three times. It was a risk, but to cross the eddy line, he'd need power more than buoyancy. He angled at the eddy, put his head down and swam as hard as the current and his sudden, hot anger could propel him.

When he hit the eddy line, it was like piling into a wall.

Jon had felt eddy lines spin and yank at him before, but he'd never felt water behave like a solid object. The impact spun him back out into downstream current. For a moment, Jon couldn't believe it had happened. He kept trying to break in even as it became obvious that nothing he did impacted his being shoved inexorably back.

The next eddy repelled him too, and again it was almost impossible to believe that water could behave like a wall. The next eddy did too, and the next, and the next. Each time he found himself shoved back, his disbelief compounded until finally the impossible had to be accepted. Things that normally worked didn't today.

He scanned the canyon walls downstream for his next chance. They were opening up a little. That would help. And if he wasn't mistaken, that cliff downstream marked the mouth of French Creek. Didn't he recall that the current bent close to shore there, around a small, cliffside eddy?

Sure enough, as the low granite cliff approached, the current carried him rapidly toward it, doing the work for him. He could see the eddy he wanted. It started at the cliff. It was 15 feet wide and 100 feet long, pie-shaped with its point upstream.

But as he approached he saw that the eddy was a seething mess. The line where it met downstream current spawned violent mushrooms of water. Jon knew he shouldn't even try. What would he do in that mess, assuming he could get in? Climb out of the violent surge up a slick, wet cliff? Right.

But he couldn't help it. Shore was a boatlength away for the first time since this thing began. He swam hard at the roiling eddy. Hit the line and for an instant felt victory. He hadn't bounced off.

Then he realized something worse had happened. He was stuck fast, caught between the opposing forces of eddy and river, water pummeling him from every direction at once. He was grateful this time when the downstream current slowly won and began to force him away from the eddy. The cliff slipped past, nearly close enough to touch, and was gone.

He began experimenting with different ferry angles, differently shaped eddies, but always the result was the same. He'd rafted, duckied, swum rivers literally as long as he could remember. If you knew how to handle yourself and you understood water, you got where you needed to go, both in boats and out of them. Except today. Today he'd failed to right a capsized boat, failed to swim his friend to safety (better not think about that now) and now he was failing to save himself.

Jon suddenly noticed that he felt breathless, as though the linings of his lungs were dripping sweat. He'd had asthma all his life, so the constricted feeling didn't frighten him. He understood the warning, though. He needed to regroup, use his remaining energy more wisely. He was more tired than he'd wanted to admit.

That was when the log swept alongside. It was 25 feet long, more than three feet in diameter, and big enough that it didn't roll when Jon draped an arm across it. It had been debarked by the water, its branches smashed off and their nubs smoothed. It felt good under his hands. He would rest here and think until his breath came easy again.

Waves occasionally slapped over his head. The log itself washed beneath the river's surface near eddy lines. Jon forced himself to keep a relaxed but firm grip on his island of relative safety and ignore these distractions.

There had to be a way out of this situation. Jon did not doubt for a moment his survival or if he did, he rejected the thought so fast he didn't notice its passing, but how the hell he was going to get the job done he couldn't figure.

He had to make something happen before dark, he knew that much. In the dark he wouldn't be able to read water, see the eddies, avoid the big logs and dangerous hydraulics. Too many things could go wrong in the dark.

That left him two hours, which at his present speed meant some 20 miles worth of chances. Worse came to worse, with a little luck he'd float past Riggins before full dark. At least two awfully big rapids waited between here and there, but he'd get through them. Then at Riggins he'd attract someone's attention. Someone with a boat.

He made a new plan: He wouldn't waste any more energy on eddies made violent by the flood, not even if they were 10 feet away. He would stay with his log, save his strength for the big rapids ahead, and wait for what he could picture in his mind, a place where the canyon lay back and the flooded river could expend its strength spreading wide instead of pummeling anything in its grip.

Almost as he made his plan, he realized such a place might be approaching. Ahead he could see an enlarging slice of sky.

Jon took careful stock. He was warm in his drysuit, warmer than he would have thought a person could be after nearly an hour in cold water. He still didn't feel tired, but the slight rasp in his breathing told him not to trust that feeling. He rested, watched the canyon widen.

When he saw the eddy, he simultaneously knew it could work and that he should not waste his remaining strength if, like the others, it tried to repel him. But the river had slowed and flattened, and this pondlike eddy reached far out from shore. At the eddy's bottom, a steep bench rose toward a homestead. At the top of the eddy, where upstream current met downstream flow, the conflicted waters rubbed whirlpools into being, but these were tiny compared to the violent mushrooms and sucking maws he'd seen only minutes upstream.

A little regretfully, Jon released his log. He began to swim a sharp downstream ferry, borrowing the river's power while simultaneously angling across its flow.

After all those failures it was almost too easy. He felt his body grabbed, felt his speed slow, slow more. Then his direction of travel changed and he was in. He had been swept nearly to the bottom of the 200 foot-long eddy but he was in and drifting peacefully back up.

He let it take him. The moment was surreal: He had pictured having to claw his way from the water, battling for every inch. Instead he tiredly picked a piece of easy shoreline up ahead, waited until that spot came abreast of him, and swam the rest of the way in. It was as though somehow, when he crossed that eddy line, he'd left the monstrous flood of the last 20-odd hours and regained the Salmon he'd known all his life.

Just downstream of his eddy was a house and a cable car crossing. Jon stripped off his lifejackets and drysuit and spread the bright red suit so Craig would see it. Then he started walking toward the cable crossing. He had to find Twerp.

Twenty

Aftermath

J on's memory gets patchy after this, as though he spent the hours and days that followed half-asleep. He knows that there were people at the house below his eddy. He crossed on their cable car with one of them. He didn't question the fact that his parents were parked on the far side, as though somehow summoned by his need.

"Twerp is dead," he blurted at the faces of his mother and father. "He's in the river. We have to get him." In memory his tone is matter-of-fact. He can't remember if he told them how hard he'd tried to save their friend. Or how much harder it had been to stop trying.

He doesn't remember that he and Maryé Barker drove back upstream to look for Craig, while his father raced downstream with the cable car owner, hunting Clarence. He doesn't remember finding

Craig walking dazed down the middle of the dirt road.

He remembers that sometime later, as they drove downriver toward Riggins, they had to stop because there were people and vehicles blocking the road. Some were Clarence's friends from his Riggins days. They were saying Clarence had been pulled from the water by guides on a high water training trip. They were saying he was alive. Alive but unconscious, with a faint, thready pulse. A van had just left for the hour-long drive to the hospital at Grangeville.

Hope and disbelief warred. Could his friend really be alive? It seemed just barely possible. Jon had been in the water nine miles, which he figured at one full hour, and he was OK. But he'd been wearing a drysuit. For Clarence it had been longer, maybe 90 minutes. With no drysuit. Unconscious most of the time.

Jon has no memory of the drive to Grangeville or of hearing the final verdict: DOA. He knows he was not surprised. And that he understood what it meant for him. He would not be spared the outcome of his choices: the trip; the craft; the decision to abandon the boat and instead try to swim Clarence to shore; and somehow hardest of all, his foot pushing shore away—pushing safety away—before the flip. He figured Clarence's rescuers had discerned a pulse because they needed to feel one. He could relate.

Jon has no clear memory of that night's visit to Clarence's mother, except that he didn't want to go and did anyway, and that she seemed oddly unsurprised. Jon doesn't remember, perhaps that night, perhaps in the next days, his own younger brother screaming at him, accusing Jon of something he also half-believed—that he'd killed the family's rare and treasured friend.

He does remember hearing that Clarence's family did not want an autopsy. Nothing a coroner might be able to explain about the man's behavior in his last hour could change that hour's outcome, they said. Unlike much of the river community, the Reeces were not angry at the thought that hypothermia might have killed him, or hopeful that something else had. Pride was a good thing. A man's choices were his own. Dead was dead.

Jon's first vivid memory after he climbed from the Salmon River is of a moment days later, and does not include much about how such an odd moment came about. The memory is of some 200 people milling beside the Salmon, most in river sandals, ball caps and shorts. The river was still high and brown. They were at Spring Bar above Riggins, near where Clarence's boat and Clarence himself had been pulled from the river. Clarence's dory was there, restlessly at anchor in the surging eddy. It was stacked full of driftwood. It smelled of diesel because Jon and his brother had stopped at the gas station in Riggins on their way up to douse it. Clarence's cremated ashes were aboard. And so, it felt to Jon in that moment, was his own flood-scoured heart.

Twenty One

The Wrong Question

Whitewater guide Mike Kennedy, formerly of Nebraska and, although he didn't know it yet, soon to write an elegy he would call 'The Boatman River King,' was rowing toward the Northwest Voyageurs' boathouse downstream of Riggins when he saw a single oar slipping down the eddy line, its outline vague even though it skimmed just beneath the river's normally transparent skin.

Mike's eyes followed the oar out of sight but he said nothing to his passengers. Minutes later he nosed the 16-foot NRS raft onto the ramp so the three in the bow could crawl out, then spun the boat with a practiced push/pull of his oars. He held onto his smile long enough for the other two to climb out the stern. His customers walked up toward the changing rooms—"don't forget to stop by the gift shop, folks"—and he stowed the sticks and relaxed into an uncharacteristic bad mood.

Screw the boss. He wouldn't row another day trip tomorrow. Mike didn't mind high water and usually he didn't mind driftwood in the river. It happened every high water spring. Running with the wood, Riggins guides called it. In spring, Mike sometimes watched entire trees, peeled and polished by the river, racing alongside the rafts while nuggets and broken branches tapped at the hypalon tubes.

But this was 1996, an extreme high water year following a ten year drought. Mike had been working on the Salmon since the mid-1970's and he'd seldom seen the river as big as it had been the past week. Today it was bigger yet. He'd never seen this much waterborne wood, either. In places it looked as though a person should be able to step from the raft onto this floating wooden surface and walk to shore.

He'd also never seen anything like what had happened in his raft today. Mike could normally depend on his familiarity with every wave and rock on the Riggins day run. It was his bread and butter. He ran the stretch perhaps 50 times a season for pay and another dozen for fun. But today, in a spot that had always been flat as a pond, a strange wave had welled beside the raft. Welled and then disappeared, but not before a hunk of wood had shot from it like a spit watermelon seed. It had clocked a guest in the face, fattening her lip. Just like that, Mike's day had gone to shit.

At pre-trip safety talks, Riggins guides tell guests the truth, that part of the fun of whitewater rafting is that it looks crazier than it is. They say the riskiest part of the trip is the drive to put-in, ha ha ha. But that was not what Mike told guests who wanted to float during spring runoff, and especially not this spring.

The woman and her companions had been upset about her injury. Mike, normally soft-hearted to a fault, found this irritating. When the guests had showed up at the boathouse that morning, he'd tried to talk them out of the float. He'd told them the river was too high. They had agreed to wear helmets and leave their smallest children ashore, but that was all. They'd driven hours to go rafting, they said, and they were going rafting.

Mike had given in. In hindsight, the woman's fat lip seemed a mild enough rebuke for the disrespect, theirs and his. If the Salmon River and its rapids were toys—and his livelihood implied that they were—they were not always harmless. They were not harmless right now. But how do you explain that to people when your industry markets whitewater rivers as though they were Disneyland rides?

Mike watched from beneath his trademark straw cowboy hat as the river ticked past the company's boat ramp at a massive 96,000 cubic feet per second, twenty times its usual late summer flow. Its muscularity made him edgy, had kept him from eating breakfast this morning before work. It also called to him. If you love a river and that river is undammed, if it drains the lion's share of central Idaho, a region so big and wild that grizzly bears have managed to maintain a toehold there, you're a hypocrite not to love all of its incarnations, including this unquiet leviathan upon which, nevertheless, he was happy to turn his back for the night.

Tomorrow, without guests who demanded safety when all he could deliver was skill, maybe he and his wife and their friends could take a boatman's holiday, run the Little Salmon in his dory. He liked that thought. The Little Salmon at high flows ran like a firehose. It was so steep and narrow that for a long time it had been considered strictly a kayakers' river. Nobody thought rafts and dories could run it until Mike's former mentor, Clancy Reece, proved they could. Now, although Clancy had long ago moved back to Lewiston, rafting the Little Salmon was a locals' rite of spring.

Mike imagined the run. Shore would race by in a blur. All the eddies would be washed out so you couldn't stop, but that was fine because you didn't want to. What you wanted was to pound along, hammered by waves big enough to stand your boat up, in a river barely wider than a two-lane road, and then to tumble as though out of a bailing bucket into the mighty Salmon herself. His mood began to revive.

An hour later a car pulled into the lot. A.K. Barker and his wife, outfitters from Lewiston, were driving upriver looking for their son and Clancy, who, they said, were engaged in some kind of race with the flooding river. Sounded like Clancy to Mike.

A.K. explained that Clancy and Jon had wanted to see how many miles they could row in 24 straight hours at flood. A.K. and Maryé intended to surprise the two with cookies. They figured Jon had neglected to bring enough food. Based on what Mike had heard of Clancy's extreme friend, that sounded like Jon Barker.

Mike almost mimicked Clancy's trademark line, "Anything worth doing is worth overdoing." But with the flooding river at his back, the joke for once felt flat.

So Mike simply said he hadn't seen the two and the Barkers left, heading upriver.

The next morning the news raced through town and rippled out among the region's whitewater folk: Clancy Reece was dead. Mike spent the morning trying to believe that his teacher, the reason he'd moved from Nebraska to Idaho, had died barely 40 river miles from where he'd sat that previous afternoon brooding about respect.

Worst of all, they were saying Clancy hadn't drowned. Ninety-six thousand cubic feet per second, the river cold as ice, and Clancy's thermal protection had consisted of a rain slicker. Mike's teacher had died of hypothermia like, well, an idiot.

In guiding communities where risk is both fact and factor, competence and respect for the river are carried like talismans. Mike knew that when his guests looked at whitewater, they saw chaos.

But a good boatman saw order and opportunity. As one avenue deteriorated, others revealed themselves. That was the point of polishing your skills and honing your judgment. Skill and judgment transformed an uncontrollable environment into one of managed risk. Skill and judgment gave you the right to ride.

Yet Clancy's body was being sent home to Lewiston to be cremated, and people said his pretty, handmade dory had been left, upside down, on the rocky shore across from Salvation Hole.

That day a crew drove upriver to rescue the boat. Mike was among them, and it was when he saw the broken oarlock that he thought about the oar he'd seen in the river the previous day. Suddenly he knew it for a fact: Clancy's big hand had been on the grip of that oar and then wasn't and one by one, avenues had closed before him until, against all odds, none remained.

Riggins talked. At the Shortbranch, the Salmon River Inn, Summerville's; at river company warehouses; at the campsites, trailers and houses of guides and outfitters. When they ran out of talk, their still faces mirrored to each other the words that remained, the ones that needed not to be said.

Mike's contribution was that oar, the way it had slipped down the eddy line like a message. The telling of it made him feel better, as if having been within touching distance of Clancy's oar somehow made his friend less alone the previous afternoon.

Of course, Clancy hadn't been alone. He'd been with Barker and some other guy. Mike had never heard of the one named Craig, but Clancy had told stories about Barker. The guy sounded wild, but he also sounded like someone who would watch your back. Yet Clancy had ended up tumbling helpless as a fishing bobber down a river he knew as well as all of them put together. In light of that brutal fact, what did it matter that Mike, sitting on his ass in an eddy 40 miles downstream, saw an oar?

Nevertheless. It did matter.

But such neat coincidences belong in movies. It wasn't his old teacher's oar that Mike had seen. Likely it was a remnant of somebody's frightening high water drama, but not Jon and Clancy's. At 3 p.m. on June 9, 1996, as Mike Kennedy watched that oar slip past, Clancy Reece, Jon Barker and Craig Plummer were still 70 miles upstream, happily racing the downward arc of the hot June sun, almost finished with yet another hare-brained adventure that few outside the whitewater guiding community were ever supposed to know about, but which would now be reported in newspapers around the region, many of whose readers would shake their heads and call the entire venture foolhardy.

A week later, Mike stood in front of a microphone at Spring Bar on the Salmon River, trying to choke out a poem he had written.

A year after that, he still occasionally found chunks of the boat's chine along the river. They were easy to spot: They had been painted that blaring red Clancy had favored. Mike would row over and pick them up, then offer the story to his guests, even though he knew that for them it was local color, part of the day's entertainment. Even though the question they always asked was, why? As in, why would a man do such a thing? And that was the wrong question.

Clarence 'Clancy' Reece, 1945 - 1996

Afterword

*All stories, if continued far enough, end in death, and he is
no true storyteller who would keep that from you.*
                                        —Ernest Hemingway

Ten years ago, as I was researching this book, I paddled across
the Salmon at Six-Pack Eddy to stand beside what remained
of Clancy's dory. Below me, the river glowed bottle-green as it does
in late summer. On the far bank, the tiny town of Riggins was visible
mostly as trees, their well-watered riot as alien as jungle against the
canyon's clean, stark, straw-colored slopes.

The hull of Clancy's dory was black. Someone had tucked a row of bright little balls into the keelboard slot. They looked like a child's marble collection but they were steelhead attractors, called 'corkies.' Head swirling with the stories I'd been told and the faces of the people who'd told them, I stared at that hull for a long time and thought about endings.

Two years ago, long after I thought I had abandoned this book, I returned. This time, from my kayak, I couldn't spot the hull. I considered going ashore to learn if it was really gone, but by then I understood a powerful fact about stories: They end where you say. If I finished my story, that burned hull would always rest beside the wild Salmon River, and so would those tiny gifts.

This seemed to me a good thing, so in the winter of 2011 I completed the book.

Unlike Clancy's dory, the people in this story didn't remain where I left them ten years ago. If you'll humor me a few minutes longer, we can stand together beside that hull and watch evening fill the canyon. The gorge is narrow here. The sun has been gone from the water for hours although the peaks still glow. While we wait for those mountaintops to go dark, while the cool evening wind stirs and then begins to pour downstream, carrying the scents of high, mossy meadows and melting snowfields to the desert canyon in which we stand, I will tell you what happened to a few of these lives.

First, me: I live indoors year-round now after guiding for 12 seasons on wilderness rivers. I am grateful I got to live for a time in a world of water and sky and clean, hard, often joyful work. I am equally grateful for my current life—for the company of a good partner; the shelves crammed with good books; the slim, magical laptop; cold IPAs in the fridge and IRAs wherever it is such things can be said to exist. But I need to know people who would not want my comfortable life. Among the pocketful of touchstones I carry, these shine.

Jon Barker's father, A.K., died last year at 71. Unlike his friend and former student, A.K. was not having the time of his life when death came for him. After decades of embracing the risks that accompany travel on summer rivers and winter mountains, it was cancer that ended A.K. Barker.

Jon is now 49, a year younger than Clancy was when the man, with uncharacteristic urgency, patched and painted his beloved dory in preparation for one more adventure. Jon wears reading glasses and his hairline has drifted north. But the man is still head-over-heels in love with rivers and the land. That doesn't surprise me, but this, at first, does: He is also still in love with this idea of folding the flooding Salmon into a 24-hour day.

In 1996, Jon, Craig and Clancy had traveled only 190 miles when they capsized. They were also several hours shy of the 24 hour goal. What that means, Jon explains, is that the project he and Clancy hatched was incomplete.

It isn't now. In 2006 Jon and a guide named Tom Hoeck clocked 251.1 miles. For perspective, recall that a whitewater raft trip rarely travels much more than 20 miles in a day, and that Jon's 100-mile day stunts amaze most river folk. And yes, he's still doing those, too.

Although 251.1 miles wasn't bad, Jon hasn't yet achieved his vision, a confluence of strong oarsmen, perfect water and weather, and careful planning. When water and weather have cooperated, he often has failed to convince an oarsman to join him. "I don't have a whole lot of high water years left when I will be as strong as I want to be," he says. "I can't believe these young raft guides aren't fighting each other to do this."

That's a good touchstone ending, right? Jon Barker rows off into the sunset, Don Quixote in Converse high tops, still questing for maximum river mileage, battling not just wind and whitewater but now also the weight of accumulating years, never sure how much of what he's doing is because of his friend although, certainly in my story and probably in his, some of it is.

But among those in this book who did not stay put, it isn't Jon who most compels me, especially not now, as we stand watching night draw a curtain over this rare river.

So. Remember Jon's little sister, Devon, barely mentioned in this book? Devon had been a public school teacher and by all accounts a good one. But not long after Clancy died, she scraped together her savings and quit her job. She bought a journal and wrote on its first page, "Anything worth doing is worth overdoing."

Then she joined the professional women's freestyle kayaking circuit. Freestyle is the gymnastics of whitewater kayaking. Its athletes surf, flip and spin on waves. By the time she took the Women's World Surf Championship in 2005, she was already a two-time national freestyle winner, a professional kayaker who traveled the world, living by the seat of her paddling pants, carving her signature onto the world's most beautiful waves. She'd been a kayaker from childhood when she could fit it in, but for those years she made kayaking her life.

Devon is teaching again, but she still competes nationally and internationally. In 2011, she succeeded in bringing the Freestyle Nationals to her home state. In 2012, Nationals will again be held in Idaho. Devon will compete.

Last spring, as Devon grieved her father the way she knew how—by surfing—she ran into a friend she hadn't seen in a long time. The man had come to the riffles across from Hippie Beach on the Salmon River to fish. Hippie Beach is two hours' float from the eddy where Clancy's dory burned. The surf spot there, one of Devon's favorites, is called Peace Wave. Last fall, Devon stood on Hippie Beach, with Peace Wave at her back, and married this man. Let's call that the end.

—February, 2012, Idaho Falls, Idaho

Acknowledgments

This book would not exist without Jon Barker's time and trust. Jon, I hope you're pleased with the result.

Others whose memories enriched this story include the late John A.K. Barker, Marye' Barker, Devon Barker, Craig Plummer, Mike Kennedy, Connie Kennedy, Charles Reece, Tom Reece, Evelyn Reece, Bruce Elmquist, Gary Lane, Curt Chang, Jim Hunt, Laurie Sapp, Frogg Stewart, Ron Howell, Mark Hollon, Barry Dow, Jack Kappas, Ron Thompson, Cate Casson, and Chris and Chuck Boyd.

Technical information (but not any errors: those are mine) was supplied by many generous people, including hydrologists Betsy Rieffenberger, Jay Breidenbach, Mary Mellema, and Ron Abramovich. The Bureau of Land Management's Luverne Grussing supplied information about the Lower Salmon. The Corps of Engineers' Matt Raby helped out with the Columbia, as did Tidewater Barge Line's John Piggott. River rangers, Forest Service, Coast Guard, and BLM employees up and down the book's various rivers offered perspective and cool details. Sources about the history of modern whitewater gear include Alan Hamilton, founding owner of Aire; and Glenn Lewman, co-founder of Whitewater Manufacturing.

Of the many books I read or reread while working on this one, my favorite was Blaine Harden's thorough but readable, *A River Lost: The Life and Death of the Columbia*.

Christine Hathwell and Steve Mays meticulously read the early manuscript. Their suggestions altered and improved the book hugely. Thirty-five volunteers provided feedback on selected chapters. I can't name them all here but their generous feedback helped me keep fighting for this project long after I might have otherwise given up. Dean Miller assisted with early brainstorming and research. Dean also wrote a chapter which, although it didn't survive the book's many revisions, was cool. Bob Deurbrouck, Sherry Raskin, Barry Rabin, Leslie Wright, and Shyne Brothers helped polish the final draft, each in his or her own way.

Big Earth Publishing's Mira Perrizo, who loves books, generously shared her expertise even after she, along with nearly every other publisher on the planet, declined this one. Agent Nancy Ellis shepherded the project for part of its pre-publication lifetime with what I suspect was typical warmth and enthusiasm. DJ Calderwood created a lovely cover and was generous with feedback about other design elements.

Barry did all the things he does. And then smiled at me.

Dear reader,

This story about a man who loved rivers has, until now, been kept alive by raft guides and the few, tiny communities along Idaho's Salmon River. Now it belongs also to you. If you want to support quality independent publishing and help spread Clancy's story, here are some things you can do:

- Post your thoughts online at Amazon, Barnes&Noble, Goodreads, Library Thing, Pinterest, or wherever you like to talk about books.
- Visit *www.anythingworthdoing.com*, 'like' and then share the page with your book-loving, river-loving and adventure-loving friends.
- Link your website or blog to *www.anythingworthdoing.com*.
- If your book group selects *Anything Worth Doing*, email the author with questions.
- Contact Jo Deurbrouck at *www.jodeurbrouck.com* for readings, guest blogging, and talks.

Thank you.

Jo Deurbrouck is a former whitewater raft guide and a frequent wanderer down the rivers, up the mountains, and through the deserts, forests, and canyons of the West. She co-authored one previous nonfiction book, authored its revision, and has contributed to the *Washington Post, Christian Science Monitor, Paddler Magazine, Creative Nonfiction* and other publications. She holds a M.A. in English from Boise State University.

www.jodeurbrouck.com

Available in print and ebook from
www.anythingworthdoing.com
or your favorite bookseller.

For wholesale orders or bulk purchases,
please visit *www.sundogbookpublishing.com*
or email *sales@sundogbookpublishing.com*.

CPSIA information can be obtained
at www.ICGtesting.com
Printed in the USA
LVHW041352300119
605774LV00001B/25

9 780985 2578